Better Homes and Gardens®

Porch&
Sunroom
PLANNER

Meredith® Books
Des Moines, Iowa

Porch & Sunroom Planner
Editor: Paula Marshall
Contributing Editor: Catherine M. Staub
Designer: David Jordan
Copy Chief: Terri Fredrickson
Publishing Operations Manager: Karen Schirm
Edit and Design Production Coordinator: Mary Lee Gavin
Editorial Assistants: Kaye Chabot, Kairee Windsor
Marketing Product Managers: Aparna Pande, Isaac Petersen, Gina Rickert, Stephen Rogers, Brent Wiersma, Tyler Woods
Book Production Managers: Pam Kvitne, Marjorie J. Schenkelberg, Rick von Holdt, Mark Weaver
Contributing Copy Editor: Ro Sila
Contributing Proofreaders: Julie Calahan, Becky Danley, Dan Degan
Contributing Illustrator: Bob La Pointe
Indexer: Kathleen Poole

Meredith® Books
Executive Director, Editorial: Gregory H. Kayko
Executive Director, Design: Matt Strelecki
Executive Editor/Group Manager: Denise L. Caringer
Senior Associate Design Director: Doug Samuelson

Publisher and Editor in Chief: James D. Blume
Editorial Director: Linda Raglan Cunningham
Executive Director, Marketing: Jeffrey B. Myers
Executive Director, New Business Development: Todd M. Davis
Executive Director, Sales: Ken Zagor
Director, Operations: George A. Susral
Director, Production: Douglas M. Johnston
Business Director: Jim Leonard

Vice President and General Manager: Douglas J. Guendel

Better Homes and Gardens® **Magazine**
Editor in Chief: Karol DeWulf Nickell
Deputy Editor, Home Design: Oma Blaise Ford

Meredith Publishing Group
President: Jack Griffin
Senior Vice President: Bob Mate

Meredith Corporation
Chairman and Chief Executive Officer: William T. Kerr
President and Chief Operating Officer: Stephen M. Lacy

In Memoriam: E.T. Meredith III (1933-2003)

All of us at Meredith® Books are dedicated to providing you with information and ideas to enhance your home. We welcome your comments and suggestions. Write to us at: Meredith Books, Home Decorating and Design Editorial Department, 1716 Locust St., Des Moines, IA 50309-3023.

If you would like to purchase any of our home decorating and design, cooking, crafts, gardening, or home improvement books, check wherever quality books are sold. Or visit us at: bhgbooks.com

Contents

Discovering the Possibilities

Explore your options for a porch or sunroom.

Most houses, regardless of architectural style, can be remodeled to include a porch, establishing a graceful transition from the indoor environment to the outdoors, or a sunroom awash with light and fresh air generously supplied through ample windows and glass doors. Even a small entry portico dramatically alters a home's appearance and expands living space. Remodeling or renovating existing space brings back lost charm and adds usable space to a house, and therefore deserves as much attention to detail as a new addition.

The combination of practicality and aesthetic appeal may explain the perennial appeal of porches and sunrooms. Many people who live in homes without porches or sunrooms consider adding them. And many homeowners who do have one or the other seek ways to reconfigure, increase the size, or improve the livability with new products and accessories specifically designed to add style and convenience.

Like any home improvement project, adding or renovating these transition spaces can seem daunting. This book provides ideas and direction for all aspects of the project from the first planning stages through furnishing the finished space. These inspiring ideas for new porches and sunrooms, and expert advice that ensures you will understand the scope of the work, will get your project started and finished right.

This wide and welcoming porch features ample opportunities to relax and enjoy an afternoon. Substantial, sturdy columns offer an expansive view. A ceiling fan circulates air when breezes languish. The sunroom beyond offers a light-filled, comfortable retreat year-round, even when it is too chilly to enjoy the open porch.

Selecting the Right Location

This sunroom addition is nestled under a giant oak. Shade from the tree during the summer and early fall offers natural cooling. After the leaves fall, the added sunlight helps warm the interior.

Identifying the best location for a new porch or sunroom is critical to your enjoyment and use of the space. Your plans for using the porch or sunroom will help you determine the best placement. If you want an open porch on which to visit with neighbors, a front porch addition is a natural choice. A location at the back of the house may prove more suitable if you envision your sunroom as a breakfast nook; siting it adjacent to the kitchen or dining room is logical. You also need to consider property size, easements, setbacks, and whether adequate space exists in what first appears to be a logical location.

For both sunrooms and porches, consider orientation to the sun and weather conditions. The best placement of the space may end up being a compromise between vistas and sunlight exposure.

In northern climates, if your goal is a sun-drenched room in which to warm yourself during long, cold winters, the sunroom should have at least one south-facing wall to take advantage of winter sun. A sunroom occupying the southeast corner of a home, with window walls facing south and east, is the ideal spot. This allows the space to bask in the early morning sun when temperatures are mild and avoids the late evening summertime sun when excess heat gain is often a problem.

The porch of this Midwest house was located to provide views of a pond. The soothing view is a perfect backdrop for alfresco meals.

Outfit a sunroom with shades or blinds to give full control over the amount of sunlight that reaches the interior.

Another consideration is the exterior views. If you're lucky enough to have good scenery surrounding your home, position your new porch or sunroom to take optimum advantage of the view.

When you can see out, others can see in. Privacy issues can arise when you have a room composed mostly of glass or an open porch. You'll want to be sure that the space isn't open to the plain view of neighbors or passersby, and that it doesn't intrude on your neighbor's sense of privacy, either.

Familiarity with your particular situation is helpful—if you've lived in your house for a year or two, you probably have a good idea of how you use various rooms of the house, how traffic patterns flow through the house, and how sunlight enters each room throughout the year. With these factors and your goals for the space in mind, you will be able to select the ideal location for your porch or sunroom, the first step to increasing the enjoyment of your home.

This sunroom addition sits at the front of a cottage-style house, the best location to maximize sunlight. The sunroom expands the adjoining great-room and floods it with natural light. The original center-door entry was replaced with twin sets of French doors flanking the new sun space.

Flexibility is key to finding space for a porch or sunroom addition that will meet your needs. Begin by checking with your community's building and planning department concerning the restrictions that apply to your property (see Understanding Your Property, pages 116–117). A typical setback requirement, for example, of 15 feet in from the sides of your property lines, and 45 feet from either front or back property lines, may restrict the placement and size of your desired new porch or sunroom. Knowing all the restrictions at the beginning of the planning stage allows you to make sensible choices while working within established local construction guidelines. For example,

your initial plan may have included a wrap-around front porch. Though it easily fits in the front yard, you discover it intrudes on local setback ordinances when it turns the corner and continues along the side of your home. Knowing this in the beginning allows you to avoid the time and expense of drawing up elaborate plans that aren't a viable option.

Involve a design professional, particularly if you face extensive building restrictions. Design professionals regularly develop creative means to achieve remodeling goals while staying within the parameters of established building codes. They bring a fresh perspective to the project

Attaching this small porch onto a 20x22-foot master bedroom addition provides a private spot to view and have easy access to the adjacent garden. A porch does not need to be large to fulfill these goals, as this petite porch shows.

that may allow you to build a porch or sunroom addition where you thought it was not possible. (See Design Professionals, pages 124–125.)

Grab a piece of graph paper, a pencil, and a straightedge and begin sketching rough designs to determine your space requirements. You may initially have envisioned an expansive front porch, only to discover an intimate spot to sip coffee and read the morning paper better meets your needs. So, rather than overbuilding, you may realize that a cozy portico adequately meets your space requirements by allowing you to tuck in a cafe table and small, comfortable chair.

MAKE A PLAN

If building restrictions prevent you from building an addition to your home, you may have the option of converting an existing room to a sunroom.

Another important consideration in any new project is the existing landscape. Think about what alterations are necessary—what plants and trees, if any, may be lost, or how to cope with building on a steep slope. Certain features—such as a large tree or valuable plantings—may require a change in the shape of your design.

Also remember that sunrooms need proper orientation to the sun to create the desired effect (see Elements of Style: Sunrooms, pages 84–113).

Choosing a Screen Porch or a Sunroom

This screen porch was built on an existing deck to provide shelter for an intimate outdoor area that the entire family enjoys. The 345-square-foot addition was designed to easily be converted to a sunroom in the future.

Making the choice between adding a screen porch or a sunroom depends on several factors, the two most important being your goals for the new space and your budget. Screen porch additions are much less expensive than sunroom additions, so if a tight budget is driving your design choices, a screen porch becomes the most logical choice. Regardless, don't lose sight of your goals. If your main goal is to have a light-filled year-round space that remains warm and comfortable even when the snow is falling, only a sunroom will satisfy the goal. Better to save to build your dream, rather than be dissatisfied. If your main goal, however, is an addition that allows family and friends to enjoy alfresco dinners without insects as uninvited guests, a screen porch serves the purpose nicely.

A sunroom includes fully insulated walls and ceiling, insulated-glass windows, and can be designed to provide both heating and cooling, similar to other rooms of your house (see Finding Your Style, pages 20–51). You also have the option to design a sunroom so it remains open to the main house year-round. During winter, a properly oriented sunroom acts as a solar collector, gaining and storing heat from the sun. A sunroom is more expensive to construct than a screen porch of similar size, so keep expense in mind when considering one.

MAKE A PLAN

If your budget prevents you from building a sunroom right now, but you have the funds for a screen porch, consider designing the porch so it is ready to accept the upgrades necessary to easily convert to a sunroom later.

A screen porch typically uses less expensive components, and rather than insulated windows, doors, and walls, the porch is mostly enclosed with inexpensive screens. Depending on your goals for the use of the addition, a screen porch is delightful during warm summer days. Breezes naturally flow through the screens, cooling a shaded screen porch on even the warmest days. On cold winter days, however, even the warmth of a bright sun will not be enough to warm a screen porch to comfortable temperatures.

Keeping Sunrooms Comfortable in Summer

This sunroom is comfortable during any season. It's constructed using foam-sandwich panels that wrap the room in a blanket of superinsulation to prevent interior temperature extremes. Deciduous trees shade the room in the summer and allow in more light to warm it in winter. Awning windows can be left open to catch fresh breezes even during light-to-moderate rainfalls.

Sunrooms function as ideal spots for enjoying a chilly early spring morning or late fall afternoon without subjecting yourself to the elements. Thanks to their insulated walls, windows, and doors and supplemental heating, these quasi-outdoor rooms remain comfortably warm and bright. The space bestows a welcome refuge, taking advantage of even the most limited sunlight during long winters. But sunrooms can also be enjoyed throughout the summer—even on the hottest days—with proper planning.

Well-planned sunrooms employ several strategies to prevent them from getting too hot. For example, many windows and skylights have optional features such as built-in shades and surface coatings designed to control solar gain (see Elements of Style: Sunrooms, pages 84–113). Sunshine and heat can be controlled with window shades or blinds designed to enhance the interior decor. Fan-assisted ventilation, controlled with a thermostat, ensures a sunroom will receive fresh, cool air so you don't have to walk into a stuffy, overheated room. A well-planned sunroom takes advantage of trees and leafy vines to provide naturally cool shading. To further minimize overheating, orient the sunroom to reduce exposure to direct sun during the hottest times of the year.

More sunrooms are now being planned with solid roofs that help minimize the amount of direct sunlight reaching the interior of the room, helping keep interior temperatures under control during summertime. Homeowners are finding that with careful placement of windows, light is maximized. Consider adding a skylight if you desire overhead light or a view of the sky.

SOLID-ROOF SUNROOM

Many experts steer homeowners away from all-glass ceilings in sunrooms. Maintenance is a huge concern: Glass ceilings require frequent cleaning to remove the sun-blocking debris that naturally accumulates on a roof. Adequate cooling is a problem: Ceiling fans or an exhaust fan often can't be included. And despite advancements in energy-efficient glazing, it is still difficult to prevent solar gain from creating an uncomfortably hot interior.

Instead, many builders and remodelers suggest installing skylights to provide natural overhead light, or maximizing glass on wall spaces, so your sunroom basks with natural light even with a completely solid roof.

If you can't imagine a sunroom without a glass roof, take care to properly site it. Take advantage of shade from deciduous trees during the summer. Plan for overhead window treatments that provide welcome shade. Keep long-handled cleaning implements handy so you can keep the overhead glass from clouding over and keep glazings gleaming.

making a sunroom
comfortable on even the
hottest days.

Structural Requirements for Screen Porches

Building codes specify several requirements for additions, including porches. These requirements ensure your new porch will remain a strong, safe structure for years. For example, if your screen porch will be attached to the house, it may require a foundation and local codes will specify the minimum depth of the footings dependent on the frost line and slope at the site. Codes also specify the height of railings or knee walls should your porch be off the ground. Though screen porches are enclosed with screening, the screen itself is not sturdy enough to prevent someone from tripping and falling through the screen. Local building codes vary; however, most specify railings at least 36 inches high on porches that are more than 30 inches off the ground.

One way to comply with railing codes and create an appealing screen porch is to build low walls—knee walls—around the perimeter of the porch. These solid walls satisfy railing requirements. Knee walls have the added benefit of raising the height of your screen material, which minimizes damage to the screen. If you prefer a more open look, lattice panels or an open railing design are viable alternatives to solid knee walls.

Because this screen porch added to a turn-of-the-20th-century home is at ground level, screens can extend to the floor of the porch. The construction—featuring a beaded-board ceiling with exposed joists—lends a vintage feel to the new space.

This screen porch, featuring a cathedral ceiling with skylights, is quite formal. Knee walls—rather than a railing with balusters—are appropriate to the style of the space. Large screen openings frame views in three directions.

This charming screen porch blurs the line between solid knee walls and open balusters for the lower portion of the screen walls. White wicker furniture, flowers, and floral prints give this porch traditional character.

Depending on your local code, a framing member at the required height may be sufficient to meet code while sustaining an open look.

Once you identify and meet the code requirements for screen porches—most likely the same as for decks because a screen porch may be thought of as an enclosed deck—a multitude of design options are available to personalize your space. The size, configuration, and style all depend on your goals, personal style, home, available space, and budget. (See Elements of Style: Porches, pages 52–83, for porch options and ideas.)

Determining the Right Style for Your Home

Inspired by a French chateau dining room, this enchanting sunroom is a stylish complement to the stately brick Georgian home. A copper-clad roof and Doric columns reinforce the classical theme. The curve of the room provides an enticing transition to the outdoors.

Porches are a great way to give an ordinary house a sense of importance and distinction, but only if the porch is designed to suit the house. To design a porch that is attractive and fits in, look at houses in your neighborhood. Watch for appealing porches on houses similar in size and style to your own. Note key features, such as the overall size of the porch, the style of the posts, and the design of railings.

Sunrooms are an ideal way to expand living space in your home and create a transition between the indoors and the outdoors.

But as with any addition, the style and placement of a successful sunroom should match or integrate well with the existing house.

Porches—as well as sunrooms—that are well-matched to houses typically have similar features as the house, such as matching roofing materials and trim. Flip through magazines and books to get ideas (see Creating Architectural Harmony, pages 122–123). To create a fitting porch or sunroom addition, you'll likely need an architect to develop your plans, so it makes

Details are critical to creating a porch or sunroom addition with the right style for your home. When selecting windows, for example, match the type, style, and size of the windows to those on the main house.

sense to find one at the beginning. Share your ideas and get the architect's advice on design and materials.

As you plan, you may find it helpful to try out your ideas on paper. Begin with an elevation drawing of your house, and make photocopies of it to experiment with designs. These sketches create a good basis for talking about what you want with an architect and, later, with a builder.

You'll need working drawings to present to the local building department for approval; unless you are well-versed in architectural design, you'll need an architect to translate your ideas to working drawings. You also need these finished drawings for a building contractor to order materials and begin work. Once you're satisfied, your architect will produce a complete set of drawings for your project (see Design Professionals, pages 124–125).

Designed to appear original to the 1906 home, this new screen porch echoes the house's rounded dormers and stone detailing. Using the same roofing material and same trim color was also critical to making the addition seamless.

Adding a Porch to an Historic Home

If you are the fortunate owner of an historic home, you probably enjoy the character, charm, and style such a house provides. In order to maintain that character, style, and historic distinction, however, you are likely limited in your ability to renovate or remodel. There are varying definitions of historic homes, however, and varying restrictions as to what can be done with such a home. Some cities have historic districts, and the term "historic house" is an official designation that carries legal obligations to the owner of such a property for preserving the look of the house, especially the exterior. Alterations typically are strictly controlled by a local historic committee that reviews any proposed changes to homes within its jurisdiction.

First, determine if your home falls within these guidelines. If it does, you might want to do some investigating. Many older houses had porches at one time, and research at your local library or historical society may reveal photographs that show your house with such an embellishment. If so, you'll have evidence of an historic precedent that may persuade an historic review committee to allow a porch to be constructed. However, the committee may limit the design to what is seen in old photographs.

Also, your house or property may display physical evidence of having a porch at an earlier date. Markings or shadows of details, such as posts or railings, indicate that an original porch was removed sometime in the past. This evidence may persuade the historic review committee to allow the construction of a new porch. If your house doesn't have evidence of a previously existing porch, look through books devoted to historic residential architecture to discover houses similar to your own that include porches. Use any of these avenues to develop a convincing argument.

If you are able to add a porch to your historic home, you'll want to engage the services of an architect or professional designer to ensure your new porch is architecturally compatible with your home and neighborhood. Look for architects and designers who specialize in work with historic homes or who have portfolios demonstrating their experience with such projects.

Consider the style, colors, and details characteristic of the architectural style of your historic home when executing a porch addition. This Queen Anne Victorian is characteristic of a collection of homes known as the Painted Ladies, with detailed bright color schemes, lacy ornamental woodwork, and decorative wooden brackets.

SALVAGE SAVVY

Architectural salvage materials can help convincingly re-create the look of an historic porch. Old windows, doors, molding, and hardware have historically correct forms and dimensions and the patina of age. The best approach to finding and recycling old materials is to check architectural salvage yards, teardowns, and flea markets before your project begins. During the planning phases of the project, show your designers, architect, and contractors what you've found so they can design your finds into the project from the start. If you aren't able to find everything in salvage, historically accurate reproductions are available from catalogs and on the Internet.

Restoring this magnificent 1870s Victorian wouldn't be complete without repairing the grand porch. Old photos from the local historical society helped when designing historically accurate details.

Finding Your Style

Imaginative living spaces connect interiors to the out-of-doors.

This expansive porch offers plenty of space for relaxing in the shade on a hot summer afternoon or for entertaining a gathering for a casual alfresco dinner party. Breezy white wicker furniture and lush potted flowers and greenery add to the charm of this outdoor retreat.

The word porch conjures images of creaking rocking chairs, mild summer breezes, and lemonade. Porches take many forms, however. A porch may be a simple roofed-over deck or an elaborate Italianate portico. A fully enclosed sunroom includes insulated walls, ceilings, and floors, insulated-glass windows and doors, and a heating and cooling system. Both porches and sunrooms are designed to gather daylight and fresh air.

The design of your porch or sunroom depends on an evaluation of your needs, your budget, and your existing home and landscape. You might want a cozy getaway space that allows you to enjoy evening sunsets in privacy. In that case, a small porch attached to the back of your house may be sufficient. If you're considering a serious architectural upgrade for your home's facade, an expansive, wraparound porch is an open invitation to gracious outdoor living.

If you envision summer entertaining on your new porch, make it accessible from your kitchen and enclose it with screened panels to keep insects at bay. If you want to enjoy the sun's warmth even in winter, build a year-round sunroom.

Porches and sunrooms have the potential to be one of the most delightful areas of your home. With planning, you can take advantage of a porch or sunroom's special characteristics while adding new ideas that increase your home's livability and value.

Style Options

Porch and sunroom designs fall into **four basic styles**. Each style can be evaluated in terms of cost, complexity, and exposure to the elements. When planning your project, start with one of the basic designs, and then customize it to suit your needs and tastes. For more inspiration, you'll find plenty of ideas in the many variations of these basic styles on the following pages of this chapter.

This inviting front porch offers a cozy, sheltered seating area. The large white support columns include subtle detailing that matches the supports on either side of the upper-story windows. Oversize stone planters add weight to the front columns and provide a workable space for planting seasonal flowers.

This new home features one of the trademark welcoming features of a century-old Queen Anne Victorian—a wide, welcoming front porch. The sweeping curve, simple architectural details, and crisp white paint help to create a porch worthy of a neighborhood with traditional character.

Open Porch

The open porch is a classic, first gaining popularity with North American homeowners during the late 1800s and influencing home design for several decades. Designed as an element of social interaction, the front-facing porch lost favor during the last half of the 20th century, replaced in part by backyard decks and patios that offer more privacy. Now, as many communities are reviving the neighborhood approach to planning and design, front porches are regaining the rightful popularity they once held.

The open porch is basically a deck covered by a roof structure supported by posts. It may be elevated or near ground level. Street-facing versions typically feature wide, welcoming stairways and perimeter railings as part of the overall entrance scheme. Large porches may incorporate more than one doorway, giving interiors added dimension and possibilities. On the complexity and material requirements scale, this is one of the easiest porches to design and construct.

Built a few steps off the ground to bring it up to the same level as a new addition, this charming porch features simple columns, metal roofing, and a tongue-and-groove ceiling and floor. A ceiling fan and all-weather wicker furniture—including a porch swing—make this a comfortable spot to relax.

Having a fireplace as the centerpiece of a three-season porch helps to make this a comfortable room in all but the coldest weather. The exposed wood and rugged limestone are perfect complements to the massive scale and sturdy character of the timber-frame construction.

Three-Season Porch

The three-season porch is designed to extend a home's usable living area with a minimum of expense. By enclosing an existing solid-floor porch area with partial walls, screens, glazed windows, and a door, a homeowner gains use of the porch during inclement weather and chilly spring or fall days. An inexpensive portable space heater lengthens the use of a three-season porch.

Popular in the 1960s and 1970s, the three-season porch is no longer as common a choice as open porches, screen porches, and sunrooms. Low-cost insulated-glass windows and doors, and the relative simplicity of adding insulation to walls and ceilings have made sunrooms the porch style of choice for many homeowners.

The three-season porch still has its benefits, however. Three-season porches are designed to allow more fresh air in than a sunroom, and lend themselves to a more casual garden-room feel. Upgrades in window technology make it easy to upgrade a screen porch to a three-season porch. Vertically sliding vinyl-glazed panels that attach over screens, for example, allow you to easily control the amount of ventilation in a three-season room, and when shut completely, provide protection from chilly weather.

MAKE A PLAN

Three-season porches are versatile spaces. Depending on your needs and style, a three-season porch can lend itself to an informal garden-style approach to decorating or a more formal extension of the interior of your home. As you plan the design of a three-season addition, consider how you will use the space and choose materials and furnishings accordingly. Avid gardeners, for example, may find that a brick floor and large potting bench create a protected spot ideal for transplanting and arranging flowers. Alternatively, upholstered furnishings that coordinate with an adjacent living room expand the interior room.

There's abundant living space tucked into this narrow, front-facing three-season porch. Plenty of sun-gathering glass makes the temperature comfortable except in the coldest weather.

A front-porch addition transformed the facade of this North Carolina home. Brick, used for the porch floor and steps, pays tribute to classic Southern design—and it's easy to maintain. The floor is graded slightly to allow for easy rain runoff.

The front-facing porch hearkens to the late 19th and early 20th centuries, when most North American homes featured a wide and welcoming front facade. At that time, porches were part of the social fabric, connecting homeowners and families with the streets and surrounding neighborhoods. As street traffic increased, making vehicle noise more intrusive, the sitting porch migrated to the rear of the house, away from passing cars and trucks. Although the move makes sense, it led to several generations of houses that favored backyard patios or decks over front-facing porches.

Today the trend is reversing. Front-facing porches that add living area and

Exactly matching the brickwork, roofing, fascia, lumber dimensions, and other materials in this front-porch addition resulted in a porch that blends smoothly with the 80-year-old home.

Broad, front-facing porches are common to turn-of-the-20th-century neighborhoods. Friendly porches were integral to the social interaction of communities, inviting passersby to stop and chat at a time when foot traffic was common.

provide an emotional investment in the surrounding community are increasingly popular projects. These additions also prove to be sound financial investments by creating homes with plenty of charm and curb appeal. Many newly built homes reflect traditional design based on familiar and comforting motifs, such as the Midwestern farmhouse and the shingle-sided seaside home of the Northeast. These new homes often include porches—large, covered rooms thoughtfully integrated into the overall design.

When planning a front-facing porch, its style and dimensions are primary considerations. Because it's a prominent feature, you want it to be a seamless addition, looking as if it were an original part of your home. For this reason, consider hiring an architect or other qualified design professional to ensure your porch is well-matched to your house (see Planning with a Purpose, pages

The design, materials, colors, and style of a new porch, particularly a front porch, should seamlessly blend with the exterior of your entire home. Consider hiring an architect to ensure that when the new addition is complete, it looks as if it were integral to the original house.

This classic front porch is still supported by the original 1910 brick piers beneath white-painted columns. The painted wood floor and ceiling, porch swing, and antique wicker chairs continue the vintage theme.

114–129). A designer should advise you whether your house would look better with a simple entry porch or with no porch at all. For example, many Colonial-style houses, such as the saltbox, are designed to have a forthright, austere appearance. If architectural integrity is important, consider the visual impact a porch will have.

The front-facing porch usually is attached directly to a house without modifications to siding, windows, or doors. For a long porch, consider an additional doorway to create access from another room, but

make sure you can live with the changes in interior traffic patterns. Prefabricated porch posts, railings, balusters, and decorative brackets and trim made of wood or polyurethane are available at most home improvement centers. Choose the parts that are appropriate to the style of your home. If you don't see appropriate parts on display, ask to see manufacturers' catalogs for parts that can be special ordered.

This now-charming home began as a bland 1950s ranch that stuck out in a neighborhood full of historical homes built in the late 1800s. The homeowners planned a remodel to include the addition of a period-appropriate, inviting front porch. The new porch frames the front door and provides welcome shelter.

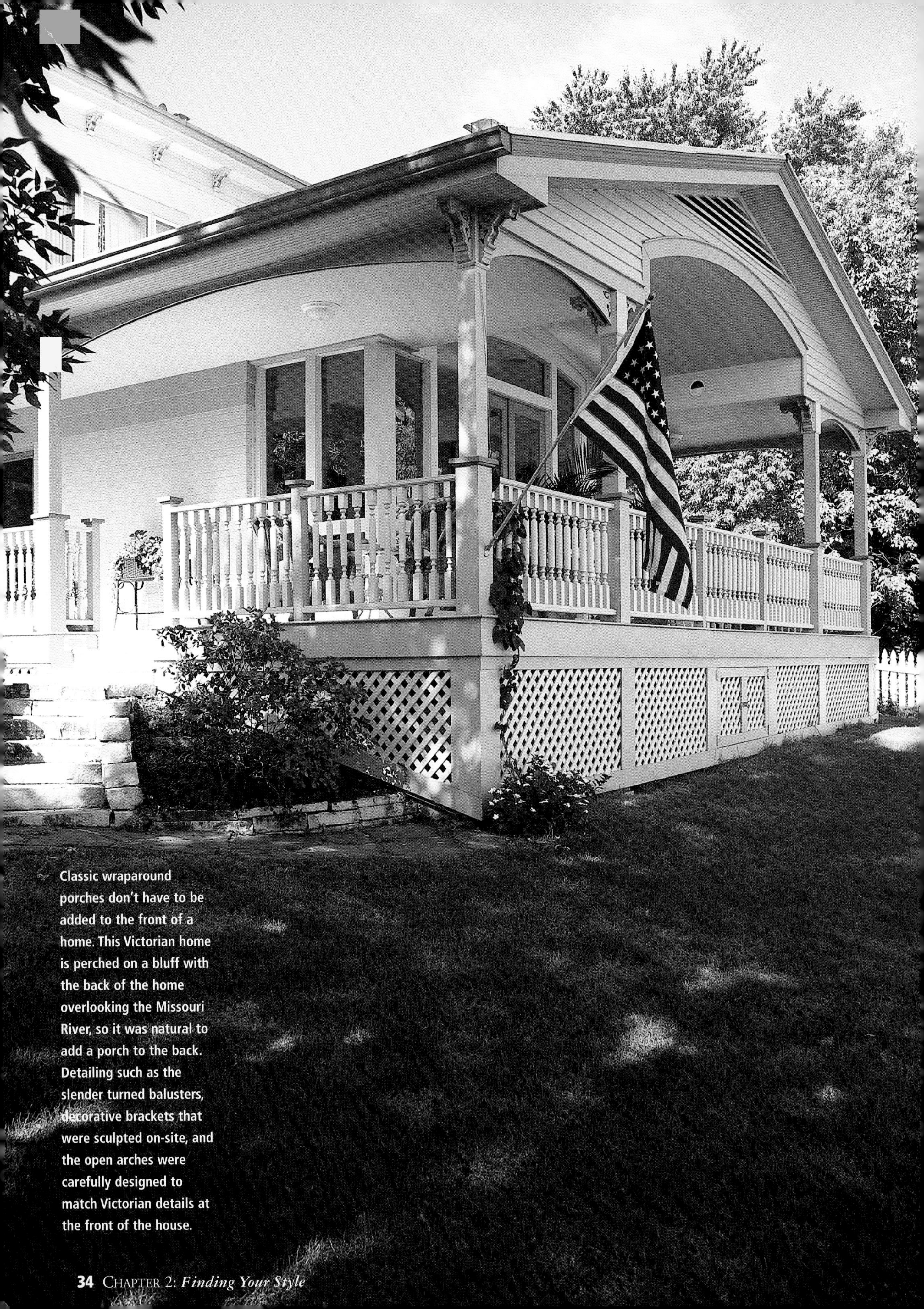

Classic wraparound porches don't have to be added to the front of a home. This Victorian home is perched on a bluff with the back of the home overlooking the Missouri River, so it was natural to add a porch to the back. Detailing such as the slender turned balusters, decorative brackets that were sculpted on-site, and the open arches were carefully designed to match Victorian details at the front of the house.

The wraparound porch is a variation of the classic front-facing porch. In this form, the porch runs along a portion of at least two sides of the house. It was popular on Victorian-style farmhouses and shingle-style bungalows of the late 19th and early 20th centuries. In terms of convenience, a two-sided porch offers flexibility. You can easily move in and out of shifting sunlight and prevailing winds, and you have a choice of views. Sit at the front if you like to watch the street-side activity, or situate yourself on the side for privacy.

A large wraparound porch generally accommodates two entrances to the house. A second stairway for a side entry is common. If you are considering a wraparound porch, plan carefully before committing to another entrance; make it a convenience—not a busy thoroughfare through what was once a quiet interior sitting area. A good example is a separate entrance to provide direct access to a master suite or an apartment. For a second entry, be sure to make the distinction between the primary, public entrance and the secondary, more private doorway. Avoid confusion with a main walkway and stairs that lead clearly and directly to the front door.

When adding a wraparound porch, a primary consideration is the setback requirement. It may not be an issue for the front-facing portion of the porch, but typically the sides of homes are closer to lot lines, especially on urban or suburban lots. Be sure to check the setback requirements in your area by calling your local building or planning department (see The Basics of Building, pages 130–137).

Even a small cottage such as this one can benefit from a wraparound porch. Hanging baskets overflowing with blooming flowers, white wicker furniture, and diminutive brackets flanking each column add to the cottage charm.

This home features a generous two-story wraparound porch. To maximize usage, both levels offer open and screened sections. Wicker furniture adorned with cushions and pillows make the screen porches a comfortable place to relax. Adirondack chairs are a weather-friendly choice for the open sections.

Porches needn't be large to be useful and appealing. Even a small entry porch—sometimes called a portico—provides shelter from the elements for visitors at the door, creates a comfortable area for sitting outdoors, and enhances the curb appeal of your home, all for minimal cost. Because the material requirements are minimal, consider using top-quality components such as finely made posts and moldings.

Although the entry porch is an especially simple addition, resist the temptation to use an existing concrete stoop or apron to support the new structure unless you've examined it carefully. Newer houses—those no more than 15 years old—may have stoops or concrete steps that have been poured as integral parts of your home's perimeter foundation. If this is the case, its foundation will extend beyond the frost line and will provide adequate support.

Older homes, however, may have stoops or concrete steps that were poured separately from the home's foundation. As a

The angled entry, wide front porch, and art-glass lunettes are throwbacks to earlier architectural eras and create a welcoming entry to this home. The covered entry porch recalls a day when neighbors dropped by more often.

A simple, functional portico was a welcome addition for this house that previously lacked any architectural styling. The tastefully designed entry is topped with a flat roof and a small, non-functional balcony. Other possibilities include curved or peaked roofs.

CREATING A USER-FRIENDLY FRONT ENTRY

Besides providing an arrival point for visitors, your front entry should also offer shelter from the elements. Adding an entry porch provides a spot for guests to take cover from the rain until you answer the door and keeps the snow from turning the morning paper to mush.

Consider these points as you plan a new front entry:

Install an outdoor ceiling fixture in the new roof overhead. Even a low-wattage outdoor bulb provides a welcoming glow and helps deter intruders.

Place house numbers near the entry and where light fixtures will illuminate the numbers at night so visitors have an easier time finding your home.

Add a simple bench or built-in seating along one side of the entry porch. It provides a place to chat with neighbors and deal with door-to-door solicitors without letting them past the front door.

This entry porch was built to shelter visitors from the wet weather in Portland, Oregon. Enough space was planned to accommodate several chairs for visiting without blocking front-door traffic. The generous use of moldings adds classical definition to this Colonial-style home.

result, they will probably shift with seasonal changes. Even slight settling may result in expensive damage to your new entry porch. An older stoop should be removed and a new concrete foundation installed, complete with piers that extend below the frost line in accordance with local building codes.

As with any other porch, an entry porch or portico should harmonize with the architectural style of your home. Include similar trim details, roofing materials, and roof pitch, and color-key it to your house. Entry porches with more than two steps or higher

than 30 inches from the ground require railings, as specified by local building codes. If the entry porch does not encompass existing exterior lighting fixtures, plan to provide lighting on the walls or in the ceiling of the new structure.

In harsh climates, consider enclosing the entry porch with windows and a storm door. This type of protection doesn't require insulated glass or supplemental heating; a three-season design is adequate for providing a sheltered area for removing wet or muddy boots and stowing umbrellas.

This variation on an entry porch actually provides shelter on a landing between stairs up from the street and stairs that lead to the main entrance to the home. The placement of this portico is a thoughtful solution to creating a welcoming entry on a severely sloped site.

A simply styled and elegant portico was a perfect addition to this small Cape Cod–styled home. The entry porch provides architectural character at a minimum investment. To ensure a stable base for the portico, a new stoop was poured and faced with brick.

French doors merge this sunroom addition with the existing kitchen. Even when the doors are closed, light from the sunroom slips into the rest of the house. Crisp white walls and woodwork and seven expansive windows brighten the room all year long. In addition to tapping into the home's furnace and central air-conditioning ducting, the room is equipped with a gas fireplace to warm even the coldest winter days.

Year-Round Sunshine

One of the best ways to bring generous amounts of light into the home and to enjoy that sunshine year-round is with a sunroom. In their most simple versions, sunrooms are available as prefabricated structures that come ready-made from the factory and are designed to attach directly to the home with few modifications to the existing siding. They are available in many sizes, shapes, and configurations to complement the architectural style of most homes. Most manufacturers also fill custom orders of sunrooms to fit unusual shapes or configurations.

An advantage of prefabricated sunrooms is the number of options available from the manufacturers. Select from wood or aluminum frames; conventional or glass roofs; variable roof pitches, wall heights, and

MAKE A PLAN

Sunrooms—whether prefabricated or a custom addition—can serve a variety of functions, depending on your needs and goals for the space. When planning, first consider how you want to use the space. Intended usage will likely impact the size, location, materials, and number and placement of windows in the sunroom. Involving a design professional in the planning process can help you create a space that will best achieve your goals.

glazing options that include insulated glass, mirrored glass, and insulated glass with inert gas fillings; and built-in shades. Match these options to your particular climate and building site. Some components, such as solid roof or floor panels, are already insulated and feature prefinished surfaces and snap-together seams that make installation fast, easy, and cost-effective.

Even for a prefabricated sunroom, most building codes require a perimeter foundation that provides support below the frost line. After the foundation is constructed and the concrete has cured, a prefabricated sunroom often is installed in only a few days.

You can also create a sunroom by building a custom addition or turning an existing space into a sunroom. Converting an existing interior room to a sun space involves replacing solid walls with windows and glass doors and, possibly installing skylights in the ceiling. Open porches and screen porches can be converted to year-round sunrooms by insulating walls and installing energy-efficient, insulated windows and doors. To ensure comfortable use of your sunroom year-round, plan for supplemental heating and cooling. This can be an extension of your existing system or independent units—such as electric baseboard heaters and window air-conditioning units (see Heating and Cooling, pages 94–99).

Stretching nearly 40 feet along the side of the house, an 11-foot-deep, prefabricated sunspace serves as both a greenhouse and a living area. Three sets of French doors open to the home's living room, providing daylight and plentiful, expansive views.

Elegance Under Glass

This more modest conservatory still provides an ideal spot to grow and enjoy flowering plants all year long. The glass-enclosed garden room provides unobstructed sun to plants that appreciate high light.

Conservatories are glassed-in sunrooms that frequently feature exceptional quality and fine details. They were popular in 18th- and 19th-century England where the mild, but often damp, climate made them a practical way to extend the outdoor season. They typically were used to grow plants in proximity to living spaces and often were referred to by the fanciful name orangerie—a place to grow orange trees. Although the methods of their construction are similar to the manufacturing of simpler, prefabricated conservatory sunrooms (see Modular Sunroom, pages 90–93), the finest versions use exceptional materials, such as hardwood frames and curved glass for roofs. Expect to pay a premium price for a high-end conservatory. Depending on the size, these conservatories range from $20,000 to $100,000, installed.

Like any ancillary structure that is attached to a main house, a conservatory must be supported by a full-perimeter foundation that extends below the frost line. After the foundation is installed, the construction is a straightforward assembly of parts.

Conservatories tend to be tall structures, often 15 feet or higher at the peak, giving them a large interior volume that needs to be considered when planning supplemental heating and cooling. Because they are all-glass structures, cooling a conservatory to comfortable temperatures in the warmest months is a big job. Most companies offer roller shades built into the roof rafters as an option to cut warming by the sun.

Consult with a heating and cooling specialist about your particular needs. An additional system, such as a small heat pump, is required to handle the heating and cooling demands of a large conservatory. To grow plants in a conservatory, plan for water-resistant flooring, such as ceramic tile, and easy access to water, such as an exterior-style spigot. If the conservatory is unheated, install a frost-proof spigot.

MAKE A PLAN

Conservatories are perfect spots for most plants to thrive—but only those plants with light needs that match the conservatory conditions. Plants that need high light require direct sun from a south, east, or west window with no obstructions from trees, buildings, or curtains. Plants that need medium light want indirect sun or bright light from a window facing east, northeast, or west.

This glass conservatory features glazings specifically designed for overhead use. Because this sunroom is located in Seattle—where the sun is often scarce—a glass-top room makes the most of muted daylight. Durable bluestone floors are a perfect surface for a room that serves a casual lifestyle.

Enclosed Patio Spaces

This screened porch offers rustic appeal and keeps bugs at bay. A portable chimenea with a stovepipe added provides warmth on chilly evenings. Check your local building codes before adding a fireplace or wood-burning stove. To create the unique floor pattern, standard terra-cotta tiles were broken into randomly shaped pieces. The pieces were laid over the existing concrete slab using conventional thin-set mortar and grouted.

If you have a ground-level backyard patio, consider enclosing a portion or all of it by adding a simple structure consisting of a roof and walls with screen panels. Screened enclosures set directly on grade level are a great way to increase your backyard enjoyment while avoiding pesky bugs (see Screening Options, pages 68–69). You won't need to install flooring—it's already there. Brick, crushed rock, flagstone, or a concrete slab work well for grade-level enclosures. The building codes in most areas, however, require that ancillary structures attached to houses be supported by perimeter foundations that extend below the frost line. An existing concrete slab typically includes a perimeter footing that will

provide adequate support. In other instances, you will need to excavate the perimeter of the proposed structure and install a code-compliant foundation. If you are unsure, have a remodeling contractor, architect, or other qualified building professional inspect your patio.

Screened structures sitting at grade level are not required by codes to provide safety railings, so the design and construction can be relatively straightforward. Vertical support members, such as 4×4s or 6×6s spaced 4 feet on center, with removable screen panels set in between, are commonly used. Not required by building codes, a horizontal safety rail, set 30 to 36 inches from the floor, prevents damage to the screen.

This screen porch is situated on a portion of an Arizona sandstone patio. Situating the porch and patio at the same level allows for seamless flow of traffic between the porch and open patio.

ELECTRICAL SAFETY

If you run electricity to a new porch structure, such as a screened-in patio (shown here) or gazebo (pages 48–49), be sure to install a ground fault circuit interrupter (GFCI) device in the line at the main electrical panel. A GFCI device interrupts current at the slightest hint of a malfunction or short circuit and is an especially good safety feature for outdoor environments where there is a risk that outlets or appliances may become damp or wet. According to the National Electrical Code, all receptacles in exposed structures should be of the GFCI variety.

A gazebo-like structure provides a perfect option for a sunroom addition to this home situated in the middle of farm country. The basic concept for the gazebo came from a grain silo. A small, enclosed hallway provides the bridge from this sunroom addition to the main house.

The circular gazebo porch at the far right of this dramatic seaside home mirrors the lines of two second-story ocean-facing porches and the curved bay of windows overlooking the deck. Adding the gazebo provided a shaded spot to enjoy the view and ocean breezes.

The Ever-Gracious Gazebo

A gazebo is usually a freestanding, decorative garden structure. While most gazebos conform to this definition, the graceful shape and beautiful style of the gazebo can be adapted as a sitting porch. Created as an extension of an existing porch, or connected to interior rooms by a short, covered passageway, the gazebo is an exceptionally charming and useful structure that lends itself to furniture groups for casual entertaining or for relaxing with the family on a summer evening.

The multisided shape and independent, conical roof of a gazebo requires clever design and careful planning to ensure it integrates well with the overall design of your house. Existing porch fascia, trim

details, railing configuration, and color schemes should be extended to an attached gazebo so that it has the appearance of having been part of the original design. Historically, gazebos are associated with English Tudor and Victorian designs. An imaginative architect, however, should be able to design a gazebo that is appropriate for your house.

An attached gazebo can be treated as an open porch or enclosed with screens (see Screening Options, pages 68–69) to create a relaxing, bug-free haven. To ensure comfort, consider running electricity to power lights, a ceiling fan, stereo equipment, or even a small refrigerator in your gazebo.

This Craftsman-inspired gazebo includes trim and other architectural detailing that makes it a natural extension of the home. The porch can be accessed from the dining room through new French doors, or through an existing door off the kitchen.

Creating Sunny Nooks

Make a sun-filled space without adding an entire room. By installing banks of windows and glass doors in smaller areas, you introduce light and fresh air to the interior of your home. Small nooks like this can light up a corridor, enliven a kitchen, or bathe a stairway landing in daylight. Instead of a full sunroom, consider a sunspace that appears as a bright surprise in your home.

A good time to consider a sunspace is when planning a remodeling project. If you are adding new walls, imagine how they might look if they were made mostly of windows. Naturally, you'll want to consider all aspects of opening up your home with glass—orientation to the sun at different times of the day and year, privacy, and views. Safety is another issue. If small children are present, limit floor-to-ceiling expanses of glass with low knee walls or by breaking up banks of windows with horizontal framing members located about 30 inches from the floor.

Like sunrooms, sunspaces take advantage of the latest innovations in window and door technology by creating beautiful

Installing a bank of operable windows a, built-in window seat, and bookcase on a staircase landing provides a sun-drenched space in which to curl up with a good book and makes an otherwise wasted space charming.

The redesign and remodel of an adjacent kitchen provided the opportunity to create this sunny mudroom that helps keep the family organized. The children stow their gear here when arriving home from school. And because the sunny nook is a welcome spot for more than storage, a small desk serves as extra work space.

MAKE A PLAN

An indoor space with a strong connection to the outdoors feels larger than its actual square footage. So you get more impact for your remodeling dollar.

When the owners of this Atlanta home wanted to renovate an attic into a master suite, they were stumped about where to locate the stairs. The solution was a stair tower added to the back of the house. The middle landing became a light-filled sunspace with a small balcony overlooking the yard. Though this space is only 7×10, it provides a high impact transition to the outdoors.

glassed-in areas that are well-insulated against heat transfer. Windows with special coatings designed to reflect heat back into rooms, high-performance glazings, and dead-air spaces filled with inert gases, such as argon, have especially good insulating capabilities—nearly as good as solid stud walls built just 20 years ago. Doors and skylights also have benefited from the technology that has improved energy performance in building components.

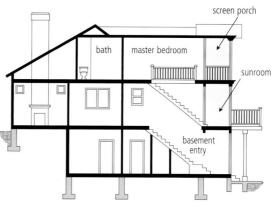

screen porch

bath   master bedroom

sunroom

basement entry

Elements of Style: Porches

Become familiar with surfaces and materials.

To turn the porch of your dreams into reality, gain a thorough understanding of all the components and how they are assembled. To begin, you'll need to decide where to access your porch from inside, choose the size and style of any windows and doors, and select materials for flooring, walls, and ceilings. Making these decisions early helps your project proceed smoothly and efficiently.

Familiarize yourself with the available options to make the wisest choices for both style and budget. Some elements, such as wood posts and railings, offer unmatched beauty and crisp details and require periodic maintenance. Other materials are expensive and can have a significant impact on your budget. To help you maintain your budget, make firm decisions about materials before construction begins.

If you work with a design professional, having definite ideas about the appearance of your porch helps the professional understand your needs, create solutions, and avoid problems. To communicate clearly, keep a scrapbook of ideas. Cut pictures from magazines and collect product brochures that illustrate colors, the materials, or the quality of workmanship that you expect.

Porches are distinctive living spaces because they are exposed to heat, cold, sun, rain, and even snow. Select weather-resistant materials and finishes that are especially designed to withstand season after season of harsh climactic conditions.

The owners of this 1920s cottage transformed a ramshackle screen porch into a charming open front porch that complements the style of their home. The simple, yet substantial columns, comfortably support a tongue-and-groove ceiling and metal roofing.

Anatomy of a Porch

Porches appear to be a less complex structure than they are: They have many components that serve specific purposes (see illustration below). It's a good idea to have a basic understanding of porch construction and terminology so you can communicate effectively with an architect, a building contractor, and other professionals involved in the design and construction of your porch.

PORCH TERMS

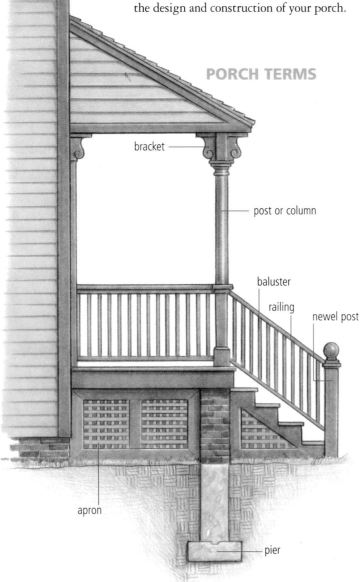

bracket

post or column

baluster

railing

newel post

apron

pier

This graceful wraparound porch was the perfect addition to re-create the charm of a Victorian turn-of-the-20th-century farmhouse. The porch sits atop wood posts supported by piers that extend below the frost line.

A simple porch built on a solid foundation veneered with stone is a perfect complement to this Arts and Crafts bungalow.

The tongue-and-groove cedar-paneled ceiling of this screen porch provided an ideal place to conceal the wiring for a ceiling fan that provides welcome air flow on even the most sultry summer days. The cedar roof panels follow the pitch of the roof, adding to the graceful shape of the porch.

Posts and Railings

Posts support the roof; the railing system—called a balustrade—runs between the posts. Local building codes determine the minimum size and the spacing of the posts. Similarly, the balustrade must comply with codes. Most codes specify a distance of not greater than 4 inches between balusters; check with your local building department before finalizing your design. After that, it's a matter of aesthetics. The size and spacing of posts should be in harmony with the architectural style of your house and the overall look of your porch addition.

Likewise, the balustrade should be designed as an integral element of the overall porch design.

Some houses, especially older homes, feature solid walls instead of railings. This is common with shingle-style homes and bungalows, where the porch is surrounded by a low-shingled wall and posts are set atop the wall. Solid walls should include scuppers—holes set at floor level to encourage drainage.

Roofs

The roof structure is another element that should harmonize with the existing

Careful integration of a porch addition to the existing house is just as important with a newer home such as this one. Thanks to careful planning and attention to detail, this screen porch looks like it was part of the original house. The porch actually began as a tiny cement-slab patio. The same shake shingles used on the main house also cover the new porch, and the shape and pitch of the porch roof coordinate with the existing bump-out to the left of the porch.

architectural style of the house. Similar fascia details, colors, and roofing materials help integrate a new porch with the house.

Like the floor framing system, the roof framing attaches to the house with a ledger. Care must be taken so that the seam between the house siding and the porch roof is sealed against leaks with flashing—a thin galvanized metal strip typically bent in an L shape (see illustration right). One leg of the flashing installs under existing siding and the other extends over the top of the new porch roofing.

The area under the roof may be left open, exposing the framing members to view from below, or enclosed. Enclosed framing has two versions: vaulted ceilings include finish materials that cover the roof rafters; a drop ceiling features ceiling joists installed horizontally and designed to carry a finish ceiling material such as wood or drywall. The classic porch ceiling material—beaded board—is a popular choice and is available as individual boards, plywood sheets, polyurethane, and aluminum panels.

Certain amenities, such as ceiling fans and lighting fixtures, install easily in porch ceilings. Plan to run the necessary wiring in the cavity between the finish ceiling and the roof.

ROOF FLASHING

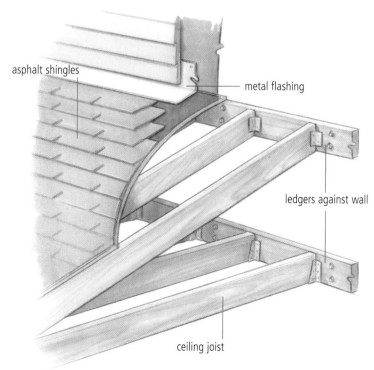

asphalt shingles

metal flashing

ledgers against wall

ceiling joist

A porch floor should be durable, resistant to moisture, and should complement the style of your porch and home. It should not warp, splinter, or chip, and it should provide a smooth, safe walking surface that is free from defects. But don't let these requirements limit your flooring choices. The options for porch floors may actually be broader than those for indoor rooms. Natural stone and woods, painted flooring, area rugs, wall-to-wall carpets, and ceramic tiles—all the standards for indoors—are available in waterproof outdoor varieties suitable for even an open porch partially exposed to the elements. In addition, materials not typically used inside, such as brick pavers, some types of stone too rough for

The bluestone floor adds a natural touch to this screen porch and holds up well against foot and paw traffic. Stability is key to masonry floors.

indoors, and poured concrete are suitable options for the porch.

The type of porch foundation generally influences flooring choices. Wood floors typically are used with post-and-pier foundations that have a substructure of beams and joists. Ceramic tile, cut stone, and brick usually are reserved for slab foundations. Tile and stone, however, can be used on elevated porches, providing the substructure is designed to withstand the considerable weight, the subfloor has been properly prepared, and the floor is pitched to shed water. Indoor-outdoor carpets install over either wood or concrete slabs. And, of course, area rugs can dress up virtually any flooring surface and foundation type.

Wood Floors

Years ago, porch floors traditionally were made using tongue-and-groove fir flooring. Fir is strong, durable, and doesn't readily warp or cup. Today, however, top-quality fir boards that are free from defects, such as knots, are increasingly rare and expensive. The tongue-and-groove boards that might serve as flooring are from softer wood species, such as pine or hemlock, and are much more prone to warping and cupping when exposed to the elements. This type of lumber also is susceptible to rot caused by moisture trapped inside the tongue-and-groove joints. For these reasons, most builders prefer not to use tongue-and-groove boards for porch flooring. A better choice is square-edge lumber that has been treated with a wood preservative or sealer prior to installation. Over time the joints between the boards will open slightly, allowing rainwater or melted snow to drip to the ground below.

All sides of each board should be coated with a preservative that is allowed to dry for two or three days before being installed. Sealer should be applied to any freshly cut ends before they are fastened to joists.

Another option is to use pressure-treated wood. This chemically treated, rot-resistant type of wood is often shipped from the factory while still moist. Bundles should be separated and the boards allowed to dry completely before installing. The color of pressure-treated wood is dull green or brown. If you want to paint pressure-treated lumber, buy kiln-dried lumber, or wait about six months for the wood to dry completely before painting.

While a natural wood finish makes an attractive floor, a painted floor adds color and some protection against the elements. Top-quality exterior paints made specifically for floors offer an especially tough finish that resists scrapes and scratches. For added durability, allow paint to dry thoroughly, then apply two coats of exterior-grade, clear polyurethane.

A handsome floor of mahogany lends rich wood tones to this New England porch. Traditionally used as the decking for ocean-going ships, mahogany is naturally resistant to moisture.

Masonry Floors

Tile, stone, and brick make excellent flooring for porches. These materials are water-resistant and are classic finishes for high-moisture areas such as bathrooms, kitchens, and mudrooms. They install readily over a concrete slab. New tile materials and installation techniques now allow tile to be used successfully even in cold climates where freeze-thaw cycles once made it difficult to keep tile in good repair in an unheated open or screen porch.

Tile and stone can be installed on elevated porches, although the additional structural materials required to support the considerable weight makes porch installation costly and rare. Refer to local building codes to determine the requirements for the

substructure. For stability and to prevent cracking grout lines, a subfloor not less than $1\frac{1}{4}$ inches thick usually is required. The thickness generally is created by using sheets of $\frac{3}{4}$-inch, exterior-grade plywood covered by $\frac{1}{2}$-inch-thick sheets of cementitious backer board—a material designed specifically for tile installations. As with any porch floor, creating a slope so that water runs away from the house is imperative.

Indoor-Outdoor Carpet and Rugs

Indoor-outdoor carpet is designed to withstand moisture and temperature fluctuations, and it is treated to resist the fading effects of ultraviolet light associated with exposure to direct sunlight. It is available in a wide variety of styles, colors, and textures. Indoor-outdoor carpet is another flooring option that allows you to create a comfortable living area in a porch environment.

This type of carpet is glued to the subfloor using a strong, water-resistant glue. Solvent-base glue generally is superior to latex-base glue because it can be applied in a wider range of weather conditions and is more water-resistant. It installs readily over concrete slabs that are dry and free from alkali residue. For porches with wood substructures, indoor-outdoor carpet requires a smooth subfloor. It can be installed over regular board flooring, but a subfloor of exterior-grade plywood is recommended. A stable plywood subfloor will help the carpet maintain its good looks for years. Waxed or oiled wood floors require resurfacing before they can be used as a subfloor for glued-down indoor-outdoor carpet.

Brick pavers bring natural charm and texture to this screen porch. Their rugged good looks and durability make them a carefree host for indoor plants and watering cans.

The painted canvas floorcloth on this screened porch creates a big, bold statement. The reds and yellows of the floor covering repeat in the fabrics used for pillows and cushions.

MAKE A PLAN

To paint your own floorcloth, buy primed canvas and acrylic paints at an art or crafts store. Mark off a simple design with artist's masking tape, then brush or stencil on your pattern. Let the canvas dry and then protect it with a coat or two of nonyellowing polyurethane.

When the homeowners upgraded an old deck to a delightful screened porch, they covered the original deck boards with outdoor carpet to keep bugs out. The carpet also provides a softer surface underfoot.

If you decide to install indoor-outdoor carpet, consider it a permanent commitment—removing it is difficult.

If your tastes change too frequently to commit to the permanence of indoor-outdoor carpet, try an area rug. Area rugs provide the opportunity to update the look of your porch easily and for relatively little expense. Sisal-look synthetic rugs can cover all or most of a porch. The newest selection of striped, solid, or whimsical-print area rugs are also waterproof. A painted canvas floorcloth is another option that can be a lively conversation piece as well as a suitable floor covering for a porch.

Painted floorboards are a durable alternative to using area rugs on a porch exposed to the elements. Use a design and colors that coordinate with the furnishings on the porch and the style and colors of your home.

PAINT PIZZAZZ

A painted floor doesn't have to just lie there; it can jump with color. Enliven your porch by creating geometric patterns with masking tape. Try experimenting with bold colors and designs. The entire floor shown here was first painted with gray-blue floor paint. A section of it—roughly the size of a typical area rug—was then divided into a pattern of squares by masking off and adding pink spaces. The design was positioned at an angle to look like an area rug. With furniture positioned at angles over the painted "throw rug," the effect is a cozy sitting area with a weather-resistant floor covering.

Walls and Screens

Porches purposely have few walls, and any existing walls or new walls should receive careful consideration to ensure they are integral to the overall design of the project. Your porch will include at least one of the following three types of walls: existing exterior walls, walls made with screening material for screen porches, and low knee walls that run around the perimeter of the porch.

Existing Walls

Exterior house walls often are covered with house siding. Generally, siding makes an attractive, durable finish and emphasizes the fact that a porch is an exterior room. Because it is already installed, it's a cost-effective wall covering. There is no need to replace siding during a porch-building project unless it is in extremely poor condition, or if replacing it is part of a larger renovation project.

A new porch will put you close to at least a portion of the home's siding. Make sure it is in good repair by replacing broken or warped wood, repainting worn surfaces, and caring for masonry by replacing missing grout and patching chipped stucco. Once repaired, the walls will be protected from sun and precipitation by the porch roof and should remain in good condition for many years.

If you don't care for the appearance of your siding, camouflage it with porch furnishings, such as shelves, and tall potted plants. Arrange seating so that it faces away from the porch walls. Add interesting details to porch posts and balustrades that draw attention away from walls. A stylish front door or a new window gives plain walls a dash of character.

The warm hue of the stucco walls on this second-floor Charleston, South Carolina, porch—or piazza—provides a pleasing backdrop for the wicker furnishings topped with inviting cushions and pillows. The solid end wall with a semicircular window affords privacy.

The expansive wall on one side of this porch makes an attractive backdrop for furniture groupings, particularly when enhanced with architectural elements.

New cedar siding was part of an exterior remodeling project that included the addition of this front porch. The upgraded siding offers a stylish backdrop for the porch, especially with decorative details such as the corbels that support a plant shelf mounted under a window.

UPGRADES FOR EXISTING WALLS

If the current siding on your home does not measure up to the quality of your new porch but replacing it is not within the budget, try these fix-up ideas:

Brick. Remove efflorescence—a white powdery substance—with water and a stiff brush. Treat brick to a new look by painting it.

Stucco. Repair cracks by filling them with acrylic silicone caulk. Caulk is available in several colors. Try to match the color of the existing stucco. If the stucco has been painted, touch up the repaired area with paint.

Vinyl or metal. Fill small holes with caulk that closely matches the color of the original siding. Use touch-up paint to disguise small scratches.

Board. Replace badly damaged or split boards to prevent water from leaking behind the boards and doing major damage to your home. Roll or spray on a protective coat of paint. Paint or opaque stains not only refresh tired-looking siding, they provide a protective shield that will prolong the life of the siding.

Any type. Accessorize. Disguise less-than-perfect existing walls by adding accessories to your porch. Some suggestions:

- Place a decorative shelf enhanced with lush plants along the existing wall.
- Hang inexpensive art that won't be damaged by humidity and moisture.
- Set up a floor screen of wood, metal, garden latticework, or bifold doors in front of a particularly offensive section of siding.
- Install window boxes under windows along the porch wall. Plant with colorful seasonal flowers.
- Display casual collectibles such as pottery, baskets, or shells on a baker's rack or on decorative shelves.

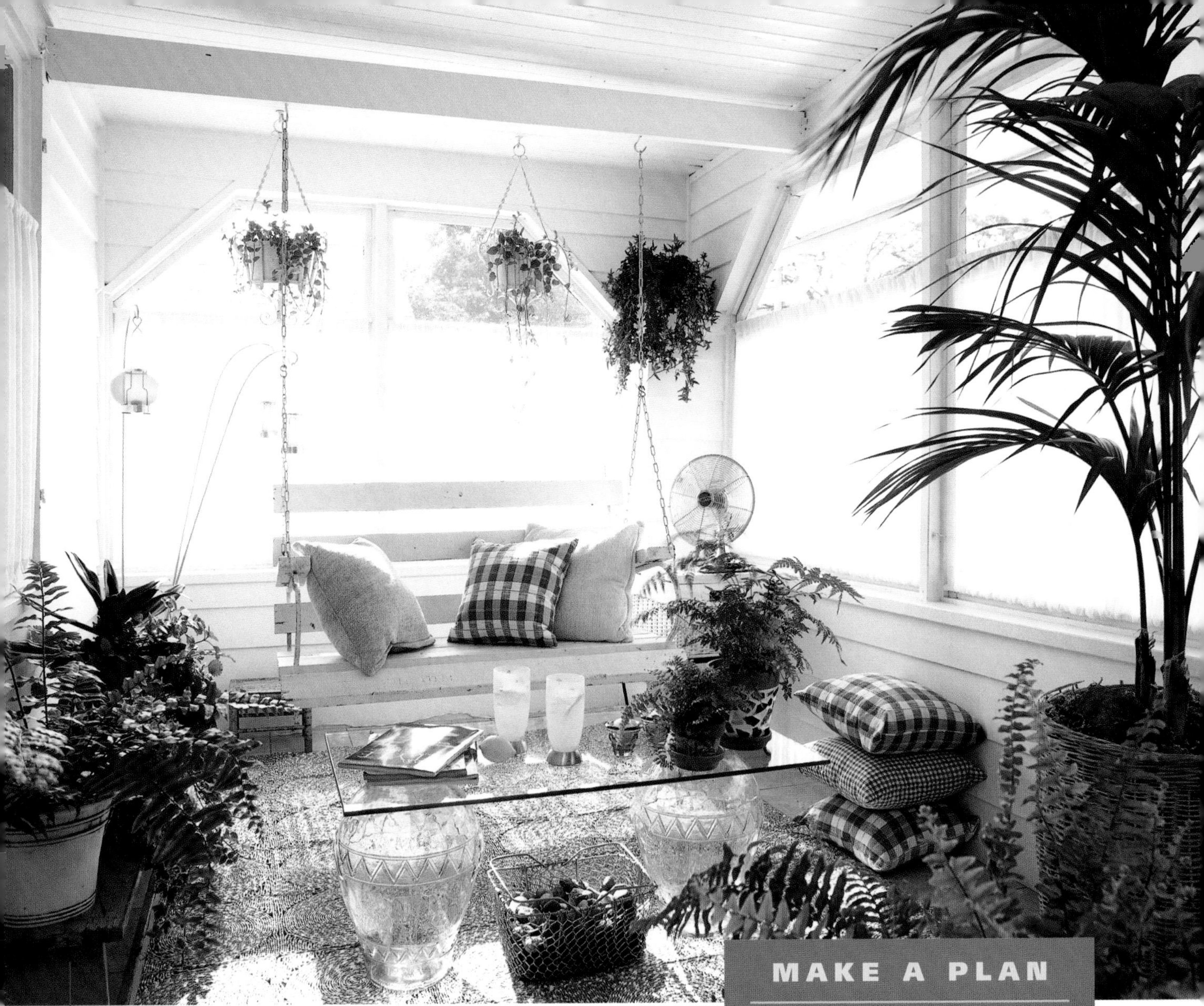

Placing screens above a knee wall helps to protect screens from dents and dings while maintaining an open, airy feel. Here, to add privacy on a city lot and protection from bright western exposure, the owner added sheer cotton panels over the fixed screens.

Screening Options

First developed in the 1800s to keep pests out of house interiors, fine-mesh insect screen is virtually unchanged from its original design. Manufactured in several widths, it can be used for seamless panels up to 60 inches wide. Consider large openings carefully—the wider the opening, the more susceptible the screen is to sagging. Openings 42 inches wide or less are recommended. Remember that small children and pets can wreck the lower portion of screened walls, and large openings increase the cost of repairs. One solution is to build low knee walls 24 to 32 inches high between the vertical structural members. Most building codes require walls or railings 36 inches high on porches with floors more than 30 inches from the ground.

MAKE A PLAN

If your screen porch has a southern or western exposure and the sun's glare is uncomfortable, look for solar shade screens that block more than 50 percent of direct sunlight while still affording ventilation and a view.

You can attach screen material directly to framing members, but a better method is to create removable screen panels. Panels should fit precisely between framing members and are held in place with clips. This way, they remove easily for repair or storage. Include storage space for screens as part of your plan.

Screen typically is made of fiberglass mesh, aluminum wire mesh, or copper mesh. (See chart opposite to compare materials.) Any of the materials will keep insects

Extending screens from floor to ceiling affords clear views in every direction. Because this screen porch is surrounded by a lush garden, the bottom screens provide the opportunity to see and smell the flowers without the bother of bugs that flowers often attract. Dividing the large expanses of screen with thin trim boards provides stability for the screening.

from invading your porch. Beyond that, selection is a matter of weighing benefits and costs. If you choose a fiberglass or aluminum wire screen, the selection of color is a matter of visual preference—dark finishes resist glare and are good choices for sunny locations.

Screening Choices

MATERIAL	PROS	CONS	COST PER SQUARE FOOT*
Fiberglass mesh	• Lightweight • Easy to work with • Won't discolor over time • Available in several colors: gray, black, charcoal	• Tendency to stretch • Won't recover original tautness if stretched • Tears easily	$0.12–$0.20
Aluminum wire mesh	• Resists corrosion • Tougher than fiberglass • Resists stretching • Resists tearing • Available in several colors: gray, black, charcoal	• Discolors over time	$0.40–$1.00
Copper screen	• Tougher than fiberglass and aluminum • Holds its shape • Coppery color that ages to a mellow brown	• Expensive • No color options	$1.50–$3.00

* Average estimated cost per square foot. Actual costs will vary.

Knee Walls

Some styles of houses include low walls, sometimes called knee walls, as part of the porch design. Shingle-style houses and Craftsman bungalows are two architectural types that typically have solid knee walls running along the porch perimeter, with support columns for the roof placed on solid, bearing portions of the walls.

Most building codes require porches more than 30 inches above the ground to be protected by railings that are at least 36 inches high and have balusters spaced no more than 4 inches apart—requirements satisfied by the construction of a knee wall. However, solid knee walls add considerable mass to the exterior of a home and should be carefully designed to fit its style. Usually this seamless appearance is accomplished by

Turn-of-the-20th-century Craftsman-style houses typically have porches with solid knee walls. This elegant beauty shows a classic finishing detail— siding material and color matched to the house.

covering the knee wall with the same exterior siding material used on the rest of the house.

To allow moisture to drain from porch flooring, solid walls should include holes or scuppers at floor level. Typically, scuppers are 2 or 3 inches high, 6 to 8 inches wide, and are spaced every 6 to 8 feet around the knee wall.

To help restore its Victorian-era elegance, the owners of this home attended to details. The knee wall—as well as the rest of the porch—features colors and detailing typical of this style of 1880s architecture.

Though knee walls can help to give a porch an enclosed, cozy feel, a low wall around the perimeter of an expansive porch such as this one is anything but confining. The lack of posts along the far end and the depth of this porch help keep it open to refreshing breezes and views.

Stairs and Railings

Stairways are one of the most important elements of a porch. They must be safe, sturdy, and good-looking. Because they project outward, they are a dramatic visual element that commands attention. During planning, give your stairway careful consideration to ensure it is a graceful and welcoming part of the overall design.

Railings are a primary safety feature of raised decks, platforms, or porches, and are a basic feature of stairways. Typically, the design of the railing system is mirrored in the balustrade of the stairway. A porch railing system includes handrails, balusters, and posts. These parts can be made of wood, high-density urethane and molded polymers, or wood covered with vinyl.

Wood offers strength and well-defined details. Although wooden porch parts typically are made from rot-resistant redwood or cedar, they require periodic maintenance with top-quality exterior-grade paint or stain. You'll find a large variety from companies that specialize in wooden parts.

MAKE A PLAN

Though traditional front porches generally feature crisp white railings and posts, consider painting trim details with colors that complement the overall exterior color scheme of your home.

Parts made from high-density urethane and molded polymers are virtually weather- and rot-proof and require little maintenance. They usually come from the factory with a baked-on white primer that can stand as the finish coat or that can be painted. They are structurally sound and meet or exceed building code requirements. These parts are made as systems that fit together with little measuring or cutting. Because they are produced in molds, there is some sacrifice in the sharpness of detail they provide.

This classic front porch features a wide stairway that provides easy access to the porch and front door, plus space for cheery potted plants. Crisp white handrails, balusters, and posts on the stairs and porch integrate the porch with the white trim on the rest of the house.

Wooden parts covered with vinyl are the least expensive and typically are available in home improvement centers. The wooden core is made with pressure-treated wood that provides strength and resistance to rot, and the vinyl coverings are maintenance-free. They come in standard sizes and may have to be adjusted on-site to fit individual porches.

One challenging element of designing good-looking railings and stairs is creating even spacing between porch posts. The design must take into account the placement of stairs with regard to the main entry door, the number of supporting posts required to hold up the porch roof, and the overall length of the porch deck. Juggling these numbers and ending up with a pleasing design is no simple task. One solution is to adjust the overall size of the porch to facilitate even spacings. Another option is to adjust the placement of one or more posts to

The exterior of this traditional home combines architectural elements from the Georgian and Federal periods. The expansive front porch features substantial columns appropriate to the visual weight of the home. A detailed railing system complements the overall look.

Porch railings typically span between columns that support the roof or between a support column and a railing post. All supports must be taken into account when planning a railing layout. In keeping with the Painted Lady Victorian exterior of this 1884 house, this porch features railings and posts detailed with rich hues.

STAIRS AND RAILINGS

The design of stairs and railings is strictly regulated by building codes. Although codes vary from region to region, most include these basic code requirements:

Raised floor surfaces (decks). Those located more than 30 inches above grade (ground) must have guardrails at least 36 inches high.

Stairs. More than 30 inches high must have guardrails at least 34 inches high, measured from the nosing of the stairs.

Guardrails. Must have intermediate rails or posts or other ornamental fill that will not pass an object 4 inches in diameter (a 4-inch ball).

Stair handrails. The height of stair handrails must be between 30 and 38 inches, measured directly above the nosing of the tread.

handrail must be installed on at least one side of a stairway that has more than two risers.

Treads. The minimum distance, measured nose-to-nose, is 10 inches.

Risers. The maximum height is $7\frac{3}{4}$ inches. A riser 6 inches high and a tread 12 inches deep are recommended for outdoor stairways. (Note: The dimensions of treads and risers cannot vary by more than $\frac{3}{8}$ inch from step to step.)

produce differences in spacings that are virtually undetectable.

Include the landing at the bottom of the stairs in your plans. This area should be integral to the overall design of the stairway. A patio or walkway made of brick, concrete, or stone forms the ideal approach to stairs. Plan the surrounding landscaping as a visual complement.

Safety was a primary concern as the homeowners were planning this porch located on a steeply sloping site. The rails feature balusters spaced closer together than code required. Because the homeowners have young children, a picket-fence style gate was added at the top of the stairs. To withstand a wet climate, the railings are made from cedar that was primed and painted.

Consider the architectural style of your home when selecting railings. The forged railing around the portico on this home is in keeping with the tradition of using ornamental ironwork with Mediterranean-style housing.

Classic porch style aligns the front stairs with the main doorway. This design of house-building makes it clear to visitors where they are to approach and enter a home. It also is the most efficient use of porch space, creating the shortest possible route from stairway to entry door and reserving the remainder of the porch area as living space. A centrally placed entry door bisects a large porch into two areas, establishing two separate outdoor living spaces. If you are planning a porch project and have the option of placing a front door in a number of locations, consider how you will use your porch. Placing the stairs and entry off to one side allows for one large area for entertaining friends and family.

Inviting Entryways

Besides leading visitors to your door by the placement of the stairs, you can paint the door a color that stands apart from the surrounding color scheme. You don't have to select a brash hue to create this effect—a solid block of contrasting color will suffice. Moldings, such as pilasters and pediments, are classic design motifs that have been used for centuries to emphasize entry doors. Another effective technique is to create a small, front-facing gable roof over the entry steps.

Large porches and wraparound designs offer the possibility of adding a second entry door. Plan second entryways carefully—they should be integrated with the interior

A series of French doors along this expansive porch help make the porch an easy extension of the indoors. The doors, with full-frame glass, visually connect the porch with the interior of the home whether the doors are open or closed. Advances in the energy efficiency of glass for exterior doors make this style of door a viable option.

Choices for Door Material

MATERIAL	CHARACTERISTICS
Aluminum	• Virtually maintenance-free • Cannot be planed, so frames must be perfectly square • Variety of colors • Embossed covers and applied moldings offer characteristics of wood • Many offer foam core to slow heat transmission
Steel	• Virtually maintenance-free • Cannot be planed, so frames must be perfectly square • Variety of colors • Embossed covers and applied moldings offer characteristics of wood • Many offer foam core to slow heat transmission
Vinyl	• Superior energy efficiency • Variety of colors • Maintenance-free • Accepts paint
Fiberglass	• Superior energy efficiency • Maintenance-free • Accepts stain to mimic wood • Lightweight
Wood	• Energy efficient • Requires periodic refinishing • Swells and shrinks with humidity changes • Preservative-treated wood offers maximum durability
Clad	• Combines energy performance of wood with low maintenance of engineered materials • Exterior clad in metal, vinyls or polyester • Interior unclad and accepts stain or paint

design and configuration of your home. A door that opens into your living or dining room will no doubt get extra use from active kids and pets with muddy feet. A better choice is to allow access to a kitchen or to create a private entry for a bedroom or home office. While you emphasize the location of your main entry, you'll probably want to de-emphasize the second, more secluded entry. Keep moldings and paint colors subtle. Remember that stairways leading directly to doors act as open invitations to approach.

Entry Doors

A porch addition gives you an opportunity to upgrade the entry door or doors that lead from the porch into your home. Entry doors are available in a wide variety of styles and types, providing a variety of design options.

And because new technologies, materials, and manufacturing techniques have improved the performance of doors, you'll appreciate the smooth operation, weather-stripped fit, high-performance insulation, and attractive hardware choices a new door offers. The characteristics of the most common entry door materials are highlighted (see Choices for Door Material, page 78).

After you have decided the location of, general style of, and material for a new entry door leading from the porch indoors, consider glazing options such as frosted and beveled glass. Installing a door with glass panes will help to visually open the transition from the porch to inside your home. Transoms and sidelights are other options for reducing the visual barrier between a porch and the indoors.

ACCESSIBLE PORCH AND ENTRYWAY

Accommodating people with special needs requires sensitive—and imaginative—solutions. This is especially true of wheelchair ramps, which may have considerable length. The architect for the historic house shown on this page had even more considerations—his final design had to meet the approval of the local historical commission. The answer is a broad porch that houses a wheelchair ramp. Because the ramp flows side to side, the depth of the porch is in keeping with the architectural style of the house. Across the front, level railings and a curb wall present the illusion of a typical elevated porch deck.

Although looks may be important, the practical concerns of creating an accessible, easy-to-use ramp are primary considerations. The basic principles of ramp design specify a slope of 1 vertical inch for every 12 inches of run for unassisted (hand-operated) wheelchair use. A doorway located 30 inches above grade would require a wheelchair ramp 30 feet long for unassisted use. If the ramp is to be used exclusively by persons with assisted (motorized) wheelchairs, a slope of 2 vertical inches for every 12 inches of run is allowed. Landings in front of doors should be at least 36 inches wide and 60 inches deep for in-swinging doors, and 60 inches square for out-swinging doors.

This new home fits into a neighborhood full of 100-year-old-homes. Classic Georgian architectural styling lends vintage character. True to Georgian tenets, the front of the house is symmetrical with a centered entry. Columns and a decorative "crown" create the portico.

Indoors flows effortlessly into outdoors through the French doors that lead from the porch through the front entry and into the kitchen. Easy access from the porch to the kitchen was essential here because family meals are eaten on the porch during nice weather.

Decorative Details

Most porches include some kind of detailing. Decorative brackets, moldings that encircle posts, and trim that enhances roof fascia are examples of details that give a porch personality and character. Porch detailing usually derives from architectural details that are copied from other parts of the house, such as brackets under an eave or moldings used to trim a dormer window. Use these visual clues as a key to selecting details that are properly scaled, visually appealing, and well-matched to the style of your house.

Some house styles use many applied details. Victorian houses are well-known for their use of complex ornamentation, often called gingerbread. There are so many individual pieces to Victorian detailing that a unique vocabulary was developed to identify each component: Fan brackets, scrollwork,

spandrels, beaded rails, and medallions are just a few of the decorative components of a Victorian porch. Although beautiful, remember that detailed trim can be expensive. If your porch project is for a Victorian house, study the possibilities carefully and compose a complete materials list before making the final decision. An architect or other professional designer can help you make choices that are in keeping with the style of your home and that won't break your project budget.

For most other houses, moderation is always a good guideline—a little bit of ornamentation can go a long way. Try simple brackets and modest trims that provide graceful accents and won't overwhelm the overall appearance of the porch. Remember that paint also can act as a decorative detail, creating interesting lines and contrasts that

Many of the details incorporated into the front porch of this new home were inspired by Victorian homes in the area. The custom porch columns were fabricated on-site from stock materials. The balustrade also features custom and stock materials combining handmade railings and purchased balusters.

are attractive and less expensive than applied moldings and trims.

As with other porch components, decorative details are made from wood and urethane or molded polymers. Wood details are available in an enormous variety of styles and sizes, and they can be custom-made to match existing details—an important consideration if you own an historic house. They usually are made from rot-resistant redwood or cedar and will require periodic maintenance with top-quality exterior-grade paint or stain.

Details made of molded polymers or urethane are durable, weatherproof, and don't rot. They can be painted to coordinate with the house colors or left with the factory white finish. They are attached like wood components—with galvanized nails or screws. They tend to be more expensive than wood parts of similar size and shape but compensate by requiring less maintenance.

The exposed beams in the gable of this porch complement the pergola on the right side of the home, and adds Arts and Crafts architectural styling to a previously bland exterior. The placement of the balusters in the balustrade continues the look.

Decorative detailing can also serve a practical purpose. The lattice with an oval cutout at one end of this porch provides a bit of privacy from the neighbors.

Elements of Style: Sunrooms

Become familiar with surfaces and materials.

The definition of the word sunroom is a bit inexact. The term simply refers to an area of the home with an abundance of windows oriented to receive a maximum amount of sun. The classic example of a sunroom is a conservatory, a space made mostly of glass—including the ceiling. Other versions include one-story rooms featuring plenty of windows, glass doors, and skylights. A third style has windows or glass doors but no overhead glazing, characteristically a sunroom on the first floor of a two-story home.

Sunrooms are similar to porches because they are often used as transition spaces between the indoor and outdoor environments. In good weather, screened sunroom windows and doors can open to breezes, creating a room similar to a screen porch. Hard-surface, water-resistant flooring, such as tile or stone, is common in sunrooms because these spaces often are used for growing plants in all seasons and must endure occasional spills. Sunrooms include heating systems that keep them warm all year—walls, ceilings, and floors must be completely insulated. Choosing proper windows and doors is an important part of your sunroom plan. Familiarize yourself with the many types of glazings and configurations available so that your sunroom is well-designed for your region of the country and your particular needs.

Outfitting a sunroom with three walls of expansive windows makes it a true transition space between indoors and outdoors. When a room contains this much glazing, it is critical to invest in insulated glass, as well as adequate heating and cooling systems for the space.

You'll find two basic options in sunroom construction: One is to build an addition or add a prefabricated model. This requires determining the proper orientation for your sunroom in regard to the movement of the sun. Also, you must find a satisfactory place to attach the sunroom to your house so that the addition is a logical extension of your living area. Most likely, you will need to knock out an existing wall or, at the least, create a doorway to your sunroom.

The other option is to turn an existing room into a sunroom by replacing solid exterior walls with windows or glass doors, and possibly adding skylights. Again, proper orientation to the sun's position throughout the year is a key factor for capturing maximum sunlight and making your sunroom the bright, cheerful place you envision.

The design of the sunroom and the configuration of the large amounts of windows, glass doors, and skylights are a matter of personal preference. Other than that, a sunroom is built using conventional construction techniques and methods. It's a good idea to have a basic understanding of sunroom construction and terminology so that you're able to communicate effectively with an architect, a building contractor, and other professionals involved in the design and construction of your sunroom.

Foundations

A sunroom must have a concrete foundation that complies with local building codes. The foundation footings must be deeper than the frost line, typically a distance of 36 to 48 inches below grade. This prevents the foundation from moving when the soil expands and contracts as it freezes during colder months.

If it is possible to build on grade, consider a slab foundation. A slab foundation works especially well as the base for tile or stone flooring—both popular choices for sunroom floors. It also is appropriate for vinyl, carpet, plastic laminate, and many types of glue-down wood flooring (see Flooring, pages 106–113).

If growing plants is an important part of your plan and your sunroom will be exposed to frequent waterings and occasional spills, consider sloping a slab floor toward a centrally located drain. A drain system requires careful planning so that the drainpipe can

SUNROOM TERMS

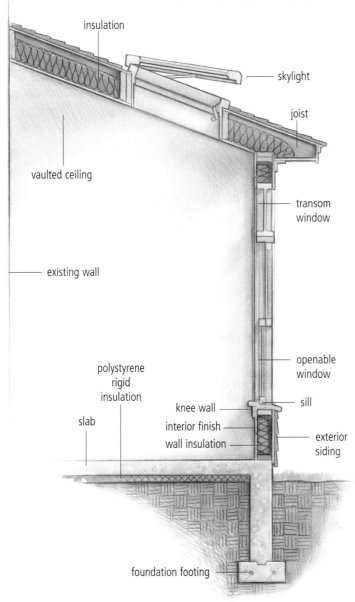

insulation

skylight

joist

vaulted ceiling

transom window

existing wall

openable window

polystyrene rigid insulation

sill

slab

knee wall

interior finish

wall insulation

exterior siding

foundation footing

This small sunroom bump-out created a sunny breakfast nook that overlooks a small but lush garden. A conventionally framed foundation supports the sunroom and aligns it with the rest of the home.

MAKE A PLAN

If your dream sunroom is just too expensive for your current budget, consider planning, budgeting, and executing the project in phases over several years. For example, in the first phase your budget may allow for the addition of an open porch. In a couple of years, you execute phase two—enclosing the porch with screening. After five years, phase three converts the screen porch to the year-round sunroom you desire. Be aware that breaking your project into stages can increase the overall cost of the project.

be tied to your existing main drain or septic system. Consulting a qualified plumber will be an essential part of your design process.

A slab floor also presents an interesting heating option. Fitted with a radiant heat system, a slab floor offers a comfortable option for home heating (see Heating and Cooling, pages 94–99). Consult with a licensed heating and cooling contractor about installing a radiant heat system in your slab floor.

If your sunroom is not directly on grade, you'll build a conventionally framed foundation consisting of concrete footings that comply with local building codes; exterior foundation walls of concrete, cement block, or wood; a framing system of girders and joists; and a subfloor. Conventionally built foundations are fairly inexpensive and straightforward to construct. The space underneath the flooring system is called the crawlspace. It is convenient for adding heating and cooling ductwork, electrical cables, and even plumbing pipes.

Though windows make a sunroom, often you'll have a solid wall between your existing living area and the sunroom. This beaded-board-covered wall continues the warm country charm found elsewhere in the room. The white wall reflects the light streaming in elsewhere in the sunroom and provides a clean, airy look.

ENERGY-EFFICIENT ALTERNATIVE

Structural insulated panels (SIPs) offer an energy-efficient, cost-effective, and strong alternative to conventional wood stud walls for sunroom additions. SIPs consist of rigid foam insulation sandwiched between two skins of oriented strand board (OSB) or aluminum, depending on the manufacturer. The rigid insulation used in SIPs is known for preventing air movement and leakage, and the solid core of insulation contains no air itself. These factors minimize drafts and eliminate vapor problems that can cause mold, both of which can be problems with conventional stick framing.

The panels are fabricated and cut at a manufacturing plant and shipped to the site in the specific sizes needed for your sunroom. Initial costs for a SIP-constructed sunroom are comparable to building with conventional wood frame construction when you factor in the savings from shorter construction time and less job-site waste because the snap-together panels arrive at the site custom-sized. It's then just a matter of connecting the panels together; panels snap together using an interlocking system. SIPs also offer a long-term cost savings because they are energy efficient.

When constructing with SIPs, consult a heating and cooling contractor who is familiar with the energy efficiency of this material. Typically your new sunroom addition will require a smaller heating and cooling system than if constructed with conventional wood stud walls.

Any type of wall surfacing can be applied to the exterior or interior of a wall constructed with structural insulated panels, offering you the same design flexibility as conventional wall construction. SIPs are also suitable for roofs and floors, as long as the foundation includes a crawl space to provide adequate ventilation.

Walls

Sunroom walls typically are framed conventionally—with wood studs, though alternative wall materials are becoming more prevalent (see Energy-Efficient Alternative, left). To maximize the insulating power of conventionally framed walls, specify 2×6 studs for more space for insulation, or use a higher R-value insulation in standard 2×4 walls. However, most of your sunroom walls will be glass—either windows or doors. Selecting high-performance glazing is one of the most important choices for your sunroom (see Windows, Doors, and Skylights, pages 100–105). Glazing should be designed to gather the most sunlight when you want it, prevent sunlight from entering the sunroom when you don't, and retain heat during winter months, especially at night.

Roofs

With the exception of all-glass conservatories or prefabricated sunspaces, sunroom roofs typically are framed conventionally, using joists of appropriate size and spacing. Design roofs with as much insulation as possible so that during colder months the sunroom retains as much heat as possible. Structural insulated panels are an energy-efficient alternative to conventional roof framing (see Energy-Efficient Alternative, *opposite*).

The number and size of skylight openings is a matter of personal preference. Control the amount of sunlight by specifying skylights fitted with operable shades or blinds. Most skylight manufacturers offer units with many shading options and insulating capabilities.

Overhead glazings must meet requirements for safety specified by local building codes. Typically safety glass is tempered, is laminated with a plastic layer, or features wire imbedded in the glass. Standard skylights and roof windows already meet strict specifications for overhead glazing safety.

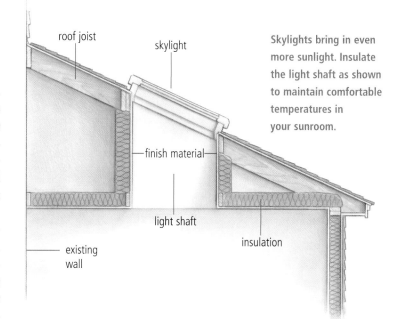

Skylights bring in even more sunlight. Insulate the light shaft as shown to maintain comfortable temperatures in your sunroom.

The homeowners wanted to create a room that was part of the house, rather than something that felt too much like an outdoor structure. The resulting space includes a stunning birch ceiling finished with a golden oak stain to accentuate the grain and match the oak woodwork throughout the rest of their home. The couple also included enough wall area between windows to avoid a glass-house effect.

A prefabricated sunroom is a relatively simple addition project. This one features a roof that matches the roof on the rest of the home, allowing it to blend seamlessly. Even small modular sunrooms must rest on a foundation that complies with local building codes.

Modular Sunroom

A modular or prefabricated sunroom can be constructed in as little as two days, depending on the size and complexity of the unit. Modular parts and framing systems simplify the process; however, the project has many facets: planning an appropriate location for the sunroom, acquiring the necessary permits, preparing the site, laying out and pouring the foundation, demolishing a portion of an existing exterior wall to provide access, and determining supplemental heating and cooling requirements. Your sunroom dealer should recommend a construction crew that is familiar with the techniques required by your type of unit, as well as a qualified contractor or subcontractors that can handle all other aspects of the job.

The type of foundation depends on the style of the sunroom and its position in relationship to your home. Grade-level sunrooms are built on slab or perimeter foundations. Typically, this type of construction includes a short perimeter wall, sometimes known as a knee or dwarf wall, that extends two to three feet above the foundation. The knee wall serves to raise the sunroom off the ground, making the joint between the unit and the foundation less susceptible to infiltration from rain or melting snow. Traditionally the wall is made of cement block or wood framing, though newer techniques make use of structural insulated panels (see Energy-Efficient Alternative, page 88). No matter the construction method, the wall often is veneered with masonry or siding that matches the existing siding of the house. A dwarf wall provides a convenient place to run electrical circuits and baseboard heaters or other types of supplemental heating and cooling devices. Wood platform foundation systems usually are used to bring a sunroom floor up to the level of an existing floor (see Flooring, pages 106–113).

If you determine that a prefabricated sunroom is the right choice for you, don't think that you're limited to a few cookie-cutter options from one dealer. Here are some suggestions to make sure that your modular sunroom will provide the results you want for years to come.

List your goals. How do you want to use your sunroom? Will it be a quiet area for relaxing off a master bedroom? Or a small conservatory for growing plants? Do you crave a sun-drenched breakfast nook to expand your kitchen? Does the whole family want a light and airy family room? Identifying the goals for your addition will help you choose the modular sunroom that is right for your needs.

Do your research. Check out websites for modular sunroom manufacturers. Most have photo galleries that allow you to view a variety of styles and options available from that manufacturer. Many also have simple planning features that allow you to put together a printable scrapbook of ideas or customize a sunroom by selecting from various options such as architectural design, shape, siding materials, window placement, and colors.

Consider aesthetics and quality. Certainly you want your new sunroom to be a beautiful addition to your home. You also want it constructed from quality materials that will make it an inviting space. Perhaps most important is the quality of glazing because windows will comprise a majority of your sunroom and can be a major source of heat loss in the winter and overheating in the summer. Look for a window company that uses low-E coatings and argon gas.

Compare what's available. Some manufacturers may specialize in a certain type of sunroom, such as conservatories. Others may offer multiple designs and architectural styles. Compare what each manufacturer has to offer with your goals and needs.

Investigate the manufacturer and the installers. How long have the companies been in the business of making and installing modular sunrooms? Ask for references and call them. Make sure other people have been satisfied with their sunroom additions. If possible, request references from both recent and long-term customers. Find out what warranties and guarantees a company offers with their products and installation and consider whether their history suggests they'll be in business long enough to honor those agreements. Once you've selected a manufacturer, try to develop a good rapport with your representative and builder.

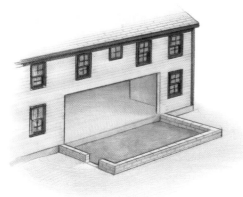

Planning a prefabricated sunroom addition typically takes advantage of existing openings to preserve traffic patterns. In this example, the deck will be removed to make way for the sunroom. The doorway will be enlarged.

After the existing deck is removed, the foundation is laid out. Block doors to prevent accidents.

A low foundation wall is one option for supporting the sunroom walls.

With the foundation set, the doorway opening can be enlarged.

When the sunroom is installed, the new walls and ceiling are sealed to the exterior siding.

Once the planning is concluded and site preparation and foundation work are completed, an access door or passageway is created between the house and the sunroom. Opening a portion of an exterior wall typically means providing temporary support for rafters or ceiling joists, disconnecting wires and pipes that run through the wall, and cutting through framing members and siding. Demolition work can be noisy, messy, and intrusive on your daily routine. Make sure your contractor is prepared to hang plastic dust curtains to protect your interiors from dirt and grime during the work. Also, make sure the contractor will adequately seal the resulting hole after work is completed so that it is secure and weatherproof. In some situations—especially when there is room to set up ladders and scaffolding, to carry materials, and to move about freely—it is possible to completely install the sunroom shell before opening the wall. This way, the opening is fully protected and secure during the renovation. Some contractors prefer not to proceed this way, however, because the ongoing work is potentially damaging to the sunroom structure.

Costs for the materials and complete installation of a modular sunroom can vary drastically depending on the size, style, and location of your home. Depending on the specifics of your sunroom, a prefabricated sunroom can cost less than $15,000 to more than $40,000.

MAKE A PLAN

Prefabricated sunrooms are available in more styles and with more options than ever. Before selecting a model or style, consider how you want to use your new sunroom space, the style of your existing home, and how the new sunroom will fit in with your existing home and yard. Then work with your sunroom dealer to make sure your choice will meet all of your needs and blend well with your home.

MAKE A PLAN

Though a prefabricated sunroom sometimes can be constructed in a matter of days, it can take weeks for the structural components to be delivered. Make sure you discuss the timeline for delivery with your sunroom dealer and account for that in your planning.

Think about how you want to use your sunroom before selecting and having a prefabricated model installed. Sunrooms are suitable to function as almost any type of room. These homeowners chose to install a soaking tub in a small, prefabricated glass bump-out that expands and enhances a bathroom. A wall of thick evergreens ensures privacy.

Heating and Cooling

Proper heating and cooling are essential for comfort in a sunroom where large expanses of glazing cause rapid heat gain and loss. Your sunroom should employ both active and passive techniques for controlling temperature fluctuations. Active techniques use mechanical systems for heating and cooling. Passive techniques use shading and ventilation to control sunlight and encourage air circulation.

Existing Mechanical Systems

If your sunroom addition is fairly modest—about 400 square feet or less—controlling the temperature is typically a matter of extending the existing heating and cooling system. Although your existing system will be sized for your present house, it probably can handle this small additional load. A larger room may require a supplemental heating and cooling unit or retrofitting your current system. A heating contractor or mechanical engineer can advise you about the feasibility of extending your present system.

To extend a forced-air system, you must add a supplemental duct to the main duct. A forced-air system also requires air-return ducts. New ducts should be properly sized for the addition and should meet all building code requirements for length and the number of turns allowed along the length. Air ducts are fairly large (typically 5 to 6 inches in diameter for round pipe and 2×12 inches for rectangular) and it is often difficult to find unrestricted routes for new ducts without tearing out portions of existing walls or ceilings. Be prepared for the added expense of renovation work to accommodate new ducts. Hot-water heating systems are easier to extend because water pipe has a small diameter (typically ½ or ¾ inches) that allows it to be easily run through joists or into existing walls.

Mechanically controlling the temperature is another consideration. If you have one centrally located thermostat, it probably means your home is set up as a single zone. A sunroom addition, with its tendency

The fireplace serves as a focal point in a sitting area arranged in this dramatic sunroom. Look for a fireplace with heat output appropriate for the size of your sunroom, and in a style that complements the design scheme for your room.

Convinced by their designer-builder that they would get more use from a sunroom than a screen porch, these homeowners added several features that provide heating and cooling options and year-round comfort. Insulating the slab floor, integrating ductwork into the concrete, and framing the screen wall sections to accept windows ensure use isn't limited to summer. The masonry fireplace provides additional warmth in chilly weather. In warm months, the custom windows are swapped for screens and the ceiling fans further circulate air.

VENT-FREE GAS FIREPLACES

Another option for heating a sunroom is a vent-free gas fireplace. These units do not require venting for safe operation. The burners are designed to reduce carbon monoxide during combustion, allowing them to be installed virtually anywhere.

Though being vent-free is a convenient feature, there are two potential drawbacks to these appliances. One specific concern is that in small rooms they may deplete oxygen to unsafe levels. For safety, manufacturers include an oxygen-depletion sensor that shuts off the appliance if oxygen falls below safe levels. Another concern is moisture. A vent-free appliance can produce a quart of water vapor per hour. To prevent unwanted condensation, a vent-free fireplace should be properly sized for your sunroom.

Although these units meet all federal safety and emissions standards, some states restrict or ban their use. Check your local building department for any restrictions that apply in your area.

Supplemental Heating and Cooling

There are many small, lightweight heating and cooling appliances that are relatively easy to add to a new sunroom. Each has a built-in thermostat and temperature-control settings. Be aware that these appliances make considerable demands on your home's electrical system. It is a good idea to consult with a heating and cooling expert or a licensed electrician about whether your supplemental heater or air-conditioner needs to be placed on its own electrical circuit.

Passive Heating and Cooling

Glassed-in sunrooms are designed to gather daylight—usually as much as possible. As a building material, glass has unique characteristics that bear on the design of sunrooms. Basically, glass permits light to pass through but doesn't let it back out. When light energy strikes solid objects, such as walls, floors, and furniture, it immediately changes into heat in a process known as heat gain. Although glass is not a great insulator, it does inhibit heat from leaving interior spaces, thus trapping the sun's heat.

Today's glass and window manufacturers have overcome the shortcomings of glass and have created products that have excellent clarity yet prevent the transfer of heat—such as double-insulated windows that are the standard of the industry. This type of glazing allows sunlight through and retains heat for long periods (see Windows, Doors, and Skylights, pages 100–105).

This all-glass conservatory features glazings specifically designed for overhead use. Located in British Columbia where the sun is scarce, a glass-top room makes the most of muted daylight. Consider a traditional roof with a skylight in areas where sunlight is the norm.

toward large temperature fluctuations, could have very different temperature requirements than other areas. What your lone thermostat determines is correct for the majority of your house may not be appropriate for the sunroom. Establish a second, thermostatically controlled zone to ensure comfortable temperatures for your sunroom. Again, consult a mechanical engineer or heating contractor about creating a second thermostatically controlled zone.

Summer

Winter

Heating and Cooling Appliances for Sunrooms

APPLIANCE	REQUIREMENTS AND FEATURES
Baseboard Heater	• Uses normal household electrical current • Available in lengths of 4 or 6 feet • Can be plugged into a wall outlet or hard-wired to an electrical circuit • Quiet • Efficient • Generally easy to conceal
Electric Wall Heater	• Uses standard household electrical current • Must be hard-wired into your home's electrical circuits • Built-in fans distribute heat • Installs between studs • Small enough to be inconspicuous • Covered with a grill or faceplate that extends about ¾ inch beyond the wall surface
Gas, or Direct-Vent, Fireplace	• Provides heat • Rated by the size of the room it can effectively heat. Determine square footage of sunroom before purchasing • Requires a natural gas line • Requires a location for a vent—usually a 3-inch-diameter pipe with an inner chamber for exhaust gases and an outer sleeve that pulls in outside air for combustion • Some types of direct-vent heaters can be thermostatically controlled • Variety of designs • In addition to heat, provides ambience
Electric Fireplace	• Provides heat • Available with variable heat settings to control temperature • Runs on standard household current • Hearth surrounds and mantels available • Some models feature separate heating elements and flames. Unit can function as space heater without displaying flames or display flames without heating room • Available with realistic imitation flames that sway and flicker
Ductless Heat Pump	• Used for both heating and cooling • Two major components—an indoor air handler and an outdoor compressor. Connected to each other by a refrigerant-carrying line that can be up to 160 feet long • Requires a hole no larger than 3 inches in diameter for refrigerant line • Ideal for conversion projects that require supplemental heating and cooling • Independent source of heating and cooling for rooms isolated on their own thermostat
Portable or Window Air-Conditioner	• Provides supplemental cooling • Rated by the square footage it can effectively cool. Determine square footage of sunroom before purchasing • Should be placed in a window or in a wall opening created just for air-conditioners so it won't obstruct daylight or views • Best distribution of cool air when placed high on a wall
Ceiling Fan	• Promotes air circulation • Variety of styles, shapes, and sizes • Generally requires headroom of not less than 80 inches from the bottom of the lowest portion of ceiling fan to the finished floor. Check local codes for specifics

Shades and other passive techniques for controlling sunlight and heat gain are important factors in creating comfortable sunroom living areas. They also help reduce the cost of operating mechanical systems that heat and cool a sunroom. Passive techniques are influenced by the seasons. In the summer, keep sunlight out during the hottest portions of the day. In winter, invite sunlight in to maximize heat gain. Spring and fall are more challenging—what begins as a chilly day can quickly turn quite warm, requiring a bit of work on the homeowner's part to establish the correct combination of passive techniques to create and maintain comfortable temperatures.

The easiest way to control sunlight is with shades, curtains, or blinds. The choice is a matter of personal preference and is often determined by the interior design of the space. Some blinds include reflective materials that bounce sunlight back through windows before it has a chance to turn into heat. Some windows and doors feature built-in blinds—the blinds are in the dead-air space between the panes of insulating glass. These types of blinds are easily controlled, allow other decorative window

Installing upper transom windows that open for ventilation allows hot air to escape from near the ceiling of this sunny sitting area. Opening the lower windows brings in cooler air.

ceiling, the better this principle will work. Vaulted ceilings work best because they channel hot air toward the highest point in the room.

Use a combination of windows and sky-lights to establish natural convection air currents. Ideally, have a row of small windows, or the lower portions of double-hung windows, serve as air intakes and a skylight to permit warm, rising air to escape. If temperature control is important (for example, if you are growing plants and need to ensure that temperatures don't get too high), consider installing a thermostatically controlled exhaust fan in the upper portion of a wall. When temperatures rise, the thermostat automatically turns on the fan, even when the household cooling system is off.

Radiant Heating

Radiant heating systems are increasingly popular because they warm the floor—not just the air circulating within a room—so that heat is delivered directly to the body's lower extremities. The result is a greater sense of warmth and comfort. Thermostats can be set to lower temperatures than with forced-air systems, thus reducing heating costs. Also, radiant systems don't require mechanical openings, such as ventilation grates, giving you greater flexibility with interior design schemes.

There are two types of radiant heating systems. Hydronic systems use tough, flexible polyethylene tubing to carry hot water through circulating coils and loops that heat floors. The tubes can be fastened to the underside of the subfloor between joists, embedded in a concrete slab, or placed on top of a conventional wood floor system and covered with a layer of lightweight concrete—an installation that requires substantial structural support to carry the weight. Hot water is furnished by a boiler or water heater. Standard systems make use of a boiler or water heater devoted to the floor heating system, though newer systems can make use of a high-efficiency hot water heater that provides water for the radiant system as well as for other hot water systems in the home. Check local building codes to

treatments to be installed, and never need cleaning. Manufacturers of skylights also offer many types of built-in shading options for their products, including roller shades, pleated blinds, and horizontal blinds.

The eaves that overhang your sunroom are another way to control unwanted heat gain. In the summer, eaves shade vertical windows during the hottest part of the day—when the sun is directly overhead. During winter, however, when the sun is lower on the horizon, eaves will not block sunlight, permitting maximum heat gain.

Another good passive strategy is to locate a sunroom so that deciduous trees—those that lose their leaves in fall—will shade the sunroom during summer. During winter, when the leaves are gone, deciduous trees will allow sunlight to warm sunroom spaces.

Natural Ventilation

Use natural convection to keep air circulating through a sunroom when weather is warm or temperate. Natural convection takes advantage of a simple principle—hot air rises. By establishing vents or window openings at low and high points within a sunroom, natural convection is used to exhaust hot, stagnant air through upper openings while introducing cooler air through lower openings. The higher your

determine whether this type of combined system is an option. Water flow and temperature are regulated by thermostatically controlled manifolds that link the runs of tubing to the heating source. Technological advances in tubing design make hydronic systems extremely reliable, and most manufacturers offer long-term guarantees against leaks or other failures.

Electrical radiant heating systems employ networks of heating cables or wires embedded in thin mats. The heating elements are protected from damage by layers of insulation and tough outer jackets made of metal or plastic. As with hydronic installations, the cables or mats may be installed underneath the subfloor, embedded in a slab, or buried in mortar. Some heating mats are designed to be installed directly under tile or stone. Other mats can be installed directly over the pad and under carpet, and directly under laminate wood floors.

Radiant heating systems installed in concrete allow the concrete to act as a thermal mass, a substance that absorbs and stores heat and releases it slowly over a period of time. The result is even, quiet distribution of heat without temperature peaks and valleys associated with forced-air systems. Concrete floors are readily covered with tile, brick, or stone—classic sunroom flooring materials that increase the amount of thermal mass available. If radiant heating is attached to the underside of a wood subfloor, the space below the heating elements is filled with insulation to ensure the heat migrates upward. Some systems include aluminum panels underneath the heating elements to reflect heat toward the living spaces.

Because the initial installation work is more time-consuming, the initial cost of a radiant heat system is substantially more than the cost of a forced-air system used to heat spaces of similar size and volume. Also, ductwork used to supply hot air for a forced-air system can be used to supply cooling; a radiant heating system must be accompanied by a supplemental cooling system. Over time, however, radiant

heating costs less to operate, reducing heating expenses. If you are interested in radiant heating, ask your heating and cooling contractor to prepare comparative bids for the two types of systems.

This sunroom boasts comfortable temperatures thanks, in part, to a pair of operable skylights on each slope of the roof.

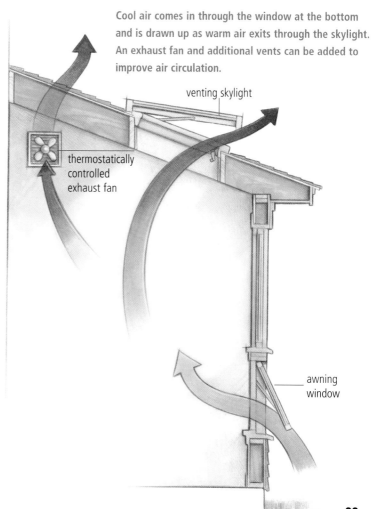

Cool air comes in through the window at the bottom and is drawn up as warm air exits through the skylight. An exhaust fan and additional vents can be added to improve air circulation.

venting skylight

thermostatically controlled exhaust fan

awning window

Glass windows and doors are primary components of any sunroom, so make them an integral part of your planning. The sizes and shapes offered by most window manufacturers are virtually unlimited and permit many possible configurations. Ideally, select windows and doors that are compatible with what you already have. For example, if your house has windows and doors with wood grilles, you will probably want to specify grilles for the new glazings installed in your sunroom.

Opening windows can turn your sunroom into a screen porch that lets in plenty of fresh air and cooling breezes. Even if all windows in your sunroom are not operable, consider installing some windows that can open near the ceiling and some that can open near the floor to provide an opportunity for air to flow through the room.

Glazing Options

Most manufacturers offer options for the type of glass used for their windows and doors. The industry standard is hermetically sealed, double-pane glass with an insulating dead-air space between the panes. This type of glazing has moderate insulating capabilities and good clarity—it transmits about 85 percent of available visible light. Standard insulating glass is a good choice for most regions of the country. High-performance glazings are available to increase energy efficiency in more severe climates. Be prepared to pay a premium price for windows and doors with specialty glazings.

• **Triple-pane glazings** include three panes of glass to create two insulating spaces for added resistance to heat loss.

• **Argon-filled windows** and doors use argon gas instead of air in the space between

Window and Door Materials

Windows and doors are made of all-wood, wood composites (a mix of shredded wood fiber and plastic resins), vinyl, aluminum, fiberglass, or wood clad with vinyl or aluminum. Each of these types offers advantages in terms of energy efficiency, maintenance, and cost.

TYPE	FEATURES
Wood	• Energy-efficient • Widely available at home improvement centers • Custom capabilities for making unusual shape windows or doors • Requires periodic refinishing • Expensive
Wood Composite	• Strength and insulating properties of wood • Less expensive than solid wood • Covered with vinyl or aluminum clad on exterior and paint primer or vinyl clad on interior • Will not accept transparent stains as wood does
Vinyl	• Superior energy efficiency • Available in a few stock colors and some custom colors • Maintenance-free • Can be painted, but will then require periodic maintenance • Moderate cost
Aluminum	• Maintenance-free • Low energy efficiency • Some include a thermal break—a material inserted into the aluminum frames to slow the transfer of heat and increase energy efficiency
Fiberglass	• Combines the stability and strength of aluminum with the insulating properties of wood and vinyl • Expensive
Clad	• Combines the energy efficiency of wood frames with maintenance-free coverings of vinyl or aluminum • Moderately priced

MAKE A PLAN

Windows are a major expense. To conserve costs, combine less-expensive fixed windows with windows that open, and use stock rather than custom sizes.

This solarium features windows that repeat the Gothic arch and diamond-shape panes that prevail throughout the rest of the home.

panes of glass. Argon is an odorless, colorless, nontoxic gas with a thermal conductivity about 30 percent lower than regular air.

• **Low-emissivity glass**, usually called low-E glass, is coated with microscopically thin layers of silver and metal oxides. It permits light to pass through the glass but helps prevent heat transfer, resulting in better heat retention in the winter and decreased heat gain from outside air in the summer. Low-E glass also blocks infrared light and most ultraviolet light—the kind of light that causes fabrics to fade—but allows about 75 percent of visible light to pass.

• **Sun glazings** are specially designed to block much of the visible spectrum, thus preventing heat gain. These types of glazings are popular in the Southwest, where days are frequently sunny and hot. Sun glazings feature reflective coatings that permit only about 40 percent of visible light to reach interiors.

• **Safety glass** is required by most building codes for skylights, large glass doors, windows within 18 inches of a floor, and windows installed on walls that incline 15 degrees or more. Safety glass is either tempered, laminated, or wire glass. Tempered glass has been specially heat treated. When it breaks, it crumbles into small bits rather than large, sharp shards. Many manufacturers offer tempered safety glass as an option for their windows and doors.

ENERGY EFFICIENCY

The National Fenestration Rating Council (NFRC) is an independent, nonprofit testing organization created by the window, door, and skylight industry to create standards of energy efficiency that can be applied to all windows (fenestration refers to any opening in a building, and usually means windows, doors, and skylights). Participation in the program is voluntary.

The NFRC does not set minimum standards of performance or draw conclusions about quality and reliability. It does, however, create a simple labeling system that allows shoppers to easily compare windows and doors in regard to thermal performance. The NFRC tests three criteria:

U-factor (how well a window keeps heat inside a home). The lower the U-factor, the more energy efficient the window.

Solar heat gain (a window's ability to block warming caused by sunlight). The higher the rating, the better the window performs at stopping solar heat gain.

Visible light transmittance (the clarity of a window). The higher the rating, the more light is admitted into a house.

R-value (a building's resistance to heat transfer). Another well-known indicator of energy efficiency is the R-value. Materials with high R-values are better insulators than those with low R-values. Most manufacturers apply this measurement to glass, although the NFRC does not offer R-value ratings.

Laminated glass has a layer of plastic film sandwiched between two layers of glass to prevent fragments from flying if the glass is broken. Wire glass is laminated with thin wires inside. If it is struck and broken, the wires prevent hands and feet from going completely through the opening.

Skylights and Roof Windows

Skylights provide an extraordinary amount of light. Because they open toward the sky, they admit 35 to 85 percent more light than vertical windows of similar size. They also allow considerable solar heat gain. To prevent sunrooms from getting too hot, equip skylights with shades or blinds. Most skylight manufacturers offer many options for shading, including pleated blinds, roller blinds, and horizontal blinds. The shading material can be either translucent or opaque. Shades that are electronically operated by a wall-mounted switch are another option,

Skylights add daylight to this breakfast area sunroom in a heavily treed yard. Blinds in the casement windows protect the room from intense summer sun at the end of the day.

MAKE A PLAN

Awning windows pivot on hinges at the top of the window frame. Though they don't open as fully as casements, awnings offer the advantage of shedding water harmlessly if left open during a rainfall. Though they can be used alone, awning windows are often installed above and/or below large picture windows to provide ventilation at the top and/or bottom of a wall.

allowing you to control the amount of sunlight at the touch of a button.

Skylight glazing options are similar to those of windows. Insulating glass is the industry standard. You can also specify low-E coatings, tints for reducing sunlight, and tempered safety glass.

There are three types of skylights:

• **Fixed skylights** cannot be opened and are usually the most economical units. Bubble-type skylights feature insulated dome-shaped Plexiglas that helps shed water.

• **Fixed, vented skylights** include a small vent that can be opened and closed to allow air to circulate. These types are less expensive than skylights that open fully.

• **Vented skylights** open with a hand crank, control rods, or electronic controls. Vented skylights are an excellent way to allow fresh air to circulate through sunrooms. It's important to equip them with an insect screen to keep out pests.

Roof windows are similar to skylights. The distinction is a matter of accessibility—skylights cannot be reached while standing on the floor, but roof windows can. Both types of units can be installed on sloped roof surfaces. Flat roofs typically require a skylight to be installed on a curb wall that is designed to prevent water from entering the opening.

A glass-crowned sunroom such as this one is the surest way to bring natural light into your sunroom. Glass-top conservatories can get uncomfortably hot, however, without careful planning. In addition to requesting low-E glass and tints to reduce sunlight, consider installing retractable shades overhead to help control the light and heat.

Windows let the sun brighten a sunroom and can also make a dramatic design statement. The half-round glazing at the peak of the roofline creates a Palladian-style window that adds strong architectural interest to the exterior of this home.

The large casement windows in this sunroom open wide to allow in plenty of fresh air and cooling breezes. The transom windows at the top are fixed but provide both additional light and architectural detail.

Installing windows from floor to ceiling ensures plenty of sunshine and wide-open views in this sunroom that functions both as a dining room and game room in a Lake Michigan beachfront home. The windows follow the pitch of the sunroom roof.

Adding a perimeter foundation to support the walls and a roof turned this former patio into a sunny three-season porch. Brick serves as a rustic and durable floor in this sunroom. Try contrasting the outdoor weathered look of brick with comfortable upholstered furniture.

made by slicing rocks or boulders into thin sheets. The surfaces are left naturally rough, called cleft or split face; honed to a dull finish with a uniform thickness; or polished to glasslike smoothness. Polished stones are more prone to scratches that eventually dull the surface, requiring periodic repolishing to maintain their glossy appearance.

Unlike ceramic tile, which is manufactured to meet certain tolerances and strengths, stone contains soft spots, cracks, and other imperfections that usually are considered to be part of the charm and character of this type of material. Some types of

stone, such as granite, are extremely hard, durable, and stain-resistant. Others, such as limestone, are much softer. Softer stones are prone to scratches and must be sealed to protect against stains. Agglomerated stone tiles are made from chips and dust left from cutting and processing various natural stone products. The waste material is bonded with a resin to make individual tiles that are then honed or polished.

When selecting stone, consult with a knowledgeable supplier about the various types of stone, the individual characteristics of each type, and the maintenance requirements.

Brick

Brick is another material traditionally associated with sunrooms. It is tough, durable, and a good transition material between outdoors and interior rooms. It is especially appropriate for sunrooms on grade, where it can be used for interior floors as well as surrounding exterior patio surfaces. Install brick over raised wood subfloors, concrete slabs, or directly on grade over a carefully prepared bed of compacted sand.

Brick is available in hundreds of colors and textures. It is rated SW for severe weathering, MW for moderate weathering, and NW for nonweathering, interior-only applications. For floors, specify paver material that has been specially manufactured to withstand the rigors of constant foot traffic. Half bricks—low-profile paver bricks about 1 inch thick—are particularly good for floor installations. They are easier to handle and can generally be installed faster than full-size brick. They reduce the overall weight of the floor, an especially important factor for brick floors installed on raised wood subfloor systems (see Masonry on Wood Subfloors, above right).

Once installed, brick flooring requires periodic maintenance to prevent staining. Use a good quality brick sealer once each year.

Sheet Vinyl and Vinyl Tile

Vinyl floor coverings are tough, moisture- and stain-resistant, and suitable for sunroom floors. They can be installed on plywood subfloors or directly over a concrete slab that has been properly cured and has a completely smooth surface that is free from defects such as cracks and chips. Both sheet vinyl and vinyl tiles are made in a wide variety of colors and patterns to match any decor. Vinyl flooring is now available in styles that mimic the look and texture of ceramic, stone, and wood floors.

Sheet vinyl is sold in 6- and 12-foot widths. The wider material means fewer seams are needed for the installation. One drawback of sheet vinyl is that damage is difficult to repair. It's much easier to replace one or two damaged vinyl tiles. However, tiles have many seams that can trap dirt or

MASONRY ON WOOD SUBFLOORS

Brick, stone, and ceramic tiles installed on a raised wood subfloor system need a firm, stable base to handle the considerable weight and to prevent flexing of the floor, which could lead to cracked materials or failed grout. Installation may require strengthening the system by doubling joists, adding support posts and piers, and making sure that the subfloor is not less than 1¼ inches thick by adding a second layer of plywood or a layer of cement backerboard. If masonry floors are part of your sunroom plans, make sure a qualified contractor or architect helps you determine the proper load-bearing capacity of your wood subfloor system.

allow moisture to get through to the subfloor. These tiles are not a good choice for high-traffic floors or for floors where spills are likely, such as in a greenhouse.

When selecting a vinyl floor, check the thickness of the wearlayer. The wearlayer is a clear layer on top of the dyes or color chips. The durability and thickness of the wearlayer determines the performance of your flooring.

Linoleum

Linoleum flooring has been making a comeback in recent years, thanks to a surge in interest in earth-friendly building materials.

When an old screen porch was remodeled to provide a sunny breakfast room, a hardwood floor that matches the home's original wood floors was installed. Because the new sunroom opens to the existing home, the consistency of flooring material was important.

Linoleum is made of natural ingredients including linseed oil, cork, limestone, wood flour, and tree resin. Another benefit of linoleum is that the color goes completely through the flooring, so if it does get scratched or gouged, the marks are less noticeable than a flooring with only a layer of color. Though the old-style linoleum of your grandmother's kitchen had a reputation for fading over time, the new linoleum features colors that stand up well over time. Because linoleum is a relatively soft surface, care does need to be taken to avoid tracking dirt or sand that can be ground into the surface.

Cork

Cork is another flooring material that can thank a surge in environmentally friendly materials for its gain in popularity. Cork flooring is made from the bark of the cork oak. This tree's bark naturally splits every 9 to 15 years and can be harvested without causing any damage to the tree. The bark

MAKE A PLAN

Consider a rubber floor. Once reserved for commercial and industrial use, rubber flooring is now available to homeowners. Rubber flooring is tough and easy to clean, making it an ideal covering for a sunroom that houses plants or sees lots of foot traffic. Rubber floors are available in sheet or tile form.

then naturally regrows. This cycle repeats for hundreds of years.

Cork floors are also a popular choice because of their characteristics. This surface is naturally warm and quiet with sound-absorbing properties. It is an excellent choice for sunrooms because it is resistant to mold and mildew and does not absorb water.

Wood

Wood flooring comes in two basic types. Solid wood flooring is one of the most

This sunroom features a durable rubber floor that is impervious to muddy shoes, spills, and paws.

popular choices for home use and features tongue-and-groove strips or planks of various types of woods, such as oak or maple. More exotic woods such as cherry, ash, or walnut cost more than traditional oak and maple. Solid wood flooring is produced in 2- to 3-inch-wide strips or 4- to 8-inch-wide planks that are either unfinished or prefinished at the factory with coats of tough polyurethane. It must be nailed or screwed to a subfloor—such as plywood. Solid wood flooring is not water-resistant and is not recommended where moisture may be present, such as the floor of a greenhouse.

Engineered wood consists of a top veneer layer of hardwood laminated to two or three layers of softwood, much like plywood. Because of the waterproof resin glue used to bond the layers and the alternating grain direction of each layer, engineered wood is much more stable and moisture-resistant than solid wood flooring. Depending on the type of product, engineered wood is either nailed down or glued directly to the subfloor. Products designed to be glued can be installed on top of a concrete slab. Some wood flooring products are installed as "floating floors." The individual pieces are glued only to each other at the edges, and the flooring is laid over a thin foam mat that absorbs footfalls and prevents the glued joints from cracking. Engineered wood is a good choice for sunrooms because of its resistance to moisture and its ability to remain stable even when temperatures fluctuate.

Laminate

Plastic laminate flooring was introduced to the U.S. building market in the mid-1990s. It is tough, durable, and resistant to moisture. It has a decorative wear layer that is bonded under pressure to a rigid core of fiberboard or particleboard. A backing material such as kraft paper or foil is added to prevent warping. A coating of aluminum oxide helps laminate flooring resist scratches, dents, stains, fading caused by sunlight, even burns from cigarettes or hot ashes. The top wear layer is created from a photographic image, allowing laminate flooring to closely mimic a variety of woods,

stone, or tile. Quality varies, so compare guarantees when shopping. The best-quality floors are warranted against defects, wear, fading, stains, and water damage for 25 years or more. Less-expensive laminate floors have 10-year guarantees.

Plastic laminate flooring installs as a floating floor—individual pieces are edge-glued only to each other and the flooring is laid over a thin foam mat. This type of flooring installs over any firm base and can be installed directly over old flooring materials such as tile, wood, or vinyl.

Concrete

Concrete is an increasingly popular choice for floors that are built directly on grade. There's no need for the additional expense of flooring materials. However, the concrete should be properly prepared to serve as a finished floor. This usually means the top surface is troweled repeatedly while it is still wet to produce a smooth, even finish.

To control cracking, concrete slabs should include seams and control joints. Seams are $\frac{1}{2}$-inch-deep grooves tooled into the surface of the concrete while it is still wet. Seams should be spaced every 3 or 4

The homeowners selected white slip-covered furniture and beige carpet for this sunroom so the fabrics and floor covering wouldn't fade in the bright all-day sunshine. The comfortable furnishings and soft floor covering help to create a bright and inviting retreat.

This brightly painted concrete floor echoes the space-defining feel of an area rug. Concrete floors are durable and easily maintained. When staining concrete, the surface must be properly prepared. The surface should be cleaned, then prepped with a commercial concrete etcher, following manufacturer's instructions and safety precautions. Then the concrete stain can be applied.

feet throughout the slab. Plan carefully to ensure that the seams are integral to the design of the flooring. Control joints prevent cracks caused by the expansion and contraction of the slab due to temperature variations. They go all the way through the concrete and are spaced every 10 or 12 feet. Typically, pressure-treated wood or felt spacers are used to make control joints. The spacer material remains in the slab.

Concrete can be dyed, painted, or acid-etched to produce a variety of interesting patterns and hues. To dye concrete, the coloring agent is added while the concrete is being mixed. This produces permanent, muted colors that extend all the way through the material. Concrete can also be colored after it is poured. Once the concrete is smoothed, a powdered color additive is sprinkled onto the surface and worked in with a trowel. Another popular method is to etch the concrete with an acid solution. For this method to work, the concrete must be cured for at least 30 days. The acid is used with pigmented coloring agents that soak into the concrete and produce a mottled, weathered look. Acid etching creates interesting textures and patterns, but the results are difficult to control. To paint concrete, choose long-wearing enamel specifically formulated for concrete floors.

After the surface is smoothed, cured, and prepared, the concrete should be sealed to protect it from spills and stains. Concrete sealer lasts many years between applications.

Carpet

Few floor finishes are as warm and inviting as carpet. It comes in an enormous array of colors, styles, and degrees of quality. New technologies make carpets more stain-resistant, longer wearing, and easier than ever to clean.

In sunrooms, resistance to fading caused by the sun's ultraviolet light is an important consideration. Carpets made from olefin are the most resistant to fading. Solution-dyed nylon also resists fading, but it is generally available only as a commercial-grade carpet.

Carpet is made from either natural or synthetic fibers. The type of fibers and the construction of the carpet determine its long-term performance.

• **Nylon** is the most popular type of carpet. It is wear-resistant, moderately priced, and available in many colors.

• **Olefin** resists staining, is color-fast, and cleans easily. It has notable resistance to moisture and mildew and is used for indoor and outdoor installations. Berber-type carpets are often made of olefin.

• **Polyester** is noted for its luxurious, soft feel, especially in varieties that feature thick, cut-pile textures. It's easily cleaned and moderately resistant to staining.

• **Acrylic** mimics wool in texture and appearance for a much lower price. It is mildew-resistant and is often used to make bathroom and small throw rugs.

• **Wool** is soft, resilient, and noted for its overall excellent performance. It is often dyed in soft, natural colors that are costly to produce and generally not available on synthetic carpets. Wool typically is more expensive than other carpets.

Flooring Material Choices

MATERIAL	ADVANTAGES	DISADVANTAGES	COST*
Carpet	• Warm, inviting look • Moderately priced • Readily available	• Shows dirt in high-traffic areas • Many carpets fade in strong-sunlight • Not good in high moisture or damp areas	$1–$50 per sq. ft.
Ceramic Tile	• Durable and low maintenance • Classic good looks • High moisture resistance	• May be cold to the touch • Unforgiving of dropped objects • Grout lines sometimes hard to clean • Moderately expensive	The price varies widely, from $1 per sq. ft. to hundreds of dollars for custom.
Concrete	• Simple material • Extremely durable and long-lasting • Eliminates need for other finish materials	• Plain, industrial look of ordinary concrete may require additional labor for coloring or painting	$4–$10 per sq. ft., installed. Coloring or acid etching is additional.
Cork	• Soft underfoot • Natural • Resists mildew • Does not absorb water	• Not suitable for high-traffic areas	$5–$15 per sq. ft.
Engineered Wood	• Has the beauty of wood but is more stable • Resists spills and moisture • Installs over many substrates	• Can't be refinished • Moderately expensive	$4–$6 per sq. ft.
Laminate	• Looks like natural material • Highly durable and resistant to stains and moisture • Installs over many substrates	• Sometimes sounds hollow underfoot • Cannot be refinished	$3–$7 per sq. ft.
Linoleum	• Made of natural raw materials • Harder and more durable than vinyl • Color goes through entire material	• Requires sealer • Cannot be left wet	Approx. $4 per sq. ft.
Stone	• Unmatched natural elegance • Almost indestructible	• Susceptible to imperfections such as cracks • Must be properly sealed • Expensive	The price varies widely, from $3 per sq. ft. to hundreds of dollars for rare types.
Vinyl	• Durable • Water-resistant in sheet form • Easy to clean • Less expensive than most other flooring choices	• Difficult to repair • Seams may permit moisture to reach subfloor • Less expensive grades may discolor with age	$1–$5 per sq. ft.
Wood	• Warm, natural appearance • Good for people with allergies	• Moderately expensive • Not good for areas where spills may occur • Needs maintenance	$5–$10 per sq. ft.

* Average estimated cost per square foot. Actual costs will vary. Installation and labor costs not included.

Planning
with a
Purpose

Establishing clear goals is the key to a great project.

Adding a wraparound porch transformed this once bland home and lends style and comfort to a space the entire family now enjoys. The new porch design needed to take into account the home's original flat facade, varying rooflines, and steep walkway. Carefully planned custom touches such as hand-chamfered railings and decorative rounded brackets give this porch Victorian styling while working with the home's existing lines.

Plan carefully to ensure that your porch or sunroom fulfills your expectations. Thorough planning involves setting clear and realistic goals, establishing a budget, being familiar with the construction process, and making informed decisions that keep the project running smoothly.

Plan in stages. First, define your primary goals. Your definition should include ideas of how you'd like to use the new space. The more precise your goals, the more satisfactory the results. For example, increasing your outdoor living space is a good objective, but if you specifically envision summer get-togethers for a group of six to eight people, you can plan a porch large enough to accommodate a good-size outdoor dining set and locate it for easy access to the kitchen or outdoor cooking area.

Once you've defined your primary goals, you'll be able to proceed through the rest of the planning stages detailed in this chapter. Use this section to learn how to choose the best location and architectural style by assessing your home and property. You'll also find out how to approach a design professional for advice. Next you'll consider the amenities needed to add a personal touch to your new porch or sunroom. Finally you'll plan a budget that will allow you to make all of this happen. After that, get ready to enjoy the space you've created.

Determine the best location for your porch or sunroom by taking a good look at your property. Make sure you take into account views, orientation to the sun, and how much privacy you'd like. Most likely, your project will alter the use of adjacent interior spaces. New doorway locations and altered traffic patterns are a few of the possible considerations. If your new porch or sunroom is part of larger, more expansive renovation plans, make sure the new spaces flow easily from one to the other and that all the changes meet your goals for comfort and livability.

Be aware of any restrictions imposed by local building departments and codes and how your proposed project will affect existing structures or important landscape features in your yard. Even a small porch must meet all the requirements set by your local planning and zoning commissions. Visit your local planning and zoning offices to pick up a plat—a map that shows your immediate neighborhood, including your property and nearby properties. The plat indicates the size and shape of your lot and shows the location of any easements—corridors established on your property that, by law, must be kept free of any structures or impediments. Several types of easements exist.

Make the most of whatever features your property offers. This porch extends over a steep slope, offering a great view from a wooded treetop perch.

• **Utility easements** provide space so that crews can access electrical power lines or other utilities to make repairs. Utility easements typically are situated at the rear of the property and may run the length of the neighborhood. They typically are 5 to 10 feet wide.

• **Overland flowage easements** include significant depressions or gullies that may collect running water during downpours or when snow melts. These physical characteristics of the land must not be altered or blocked by construction. Flowage easements prohibit structures from being built close to runoff areas where foundations may be undermined or damaged.

• **Accessibility easements** ensure that the property has direct access to a main road or byway. Creating these easements is a common practice when property is split into two parcels, creating a front-facing lot that abuts a road and a rear-facing lot that does not. An accessibility easement guarantees the rear property a corridor—usually wide enough for a driveway—by which a main road is gained.

• **Buffer easements** are created when a property abuts a public park. The buffer prevents residential construction from intruding on the character of the park.

In addition to easements, most properties are subject to setback requirements—a distance measured from the edges of the property where construction cannot take place. A typical suburban lot may have a front setback of 30 to 40 feet, side setbacks of 15 feet, and rear setbacks of 10 to 20 feet. These setbacks include the eaves—a part of the structure that's sometimes overlooked when situating an addition on a piece of property.

When you've finished designing your porch or sunroom addition, the local planning commission requires you to submit a sketch of the site plan for approval. They check the sketch against a plat map to make sure your plans don't intrude on easements or violate setback requirements. Then, the building department will check the construction plans so a building permit can be issued (see The Basics of Building, pages 130–137).

Having a challenging property can lead to innovative design ideas. This new, cantilevered porch addition takes advantage of a steeply sloped sight. The homeowners love the view from their wooded treetop perch. The underside of the porch is covered with screening to prevent the entry of insects.

MAKE A PLAN

Think creatively when considering how to situate your new porch or sunroom on your property and in relation to the current rooms in your home. Perhaps you've always pictured a sunny breakfast nook off the side of your kitchen, but easements prevent this. Rather than foregoing your plans altogether, imagine instead the alternatives. Perhaps you could position the sunroom at the back of your home and add a walkthrough pantry between the sunroom and existing kitchen. The project still provides the sunny breakfast room of your dreams, and you've added much-needed storage space too.

This sunroom includes fixtures that bounce light off the ceiling to provide a soft ambience throughout the room. The room also was wired for a ceiling fan and electrical outlets throughout to allow for flexible placement of task lights as needed.

on the bulbs themselves. A typical 60-watt lightbulb produces about 840 lumens. Figure you'll need a minimum of 10 lumens per square foot of living space. For reading and other specific tasks, a floor or table lamp with a 100-watt bulb is ideal. Always refer to the lamp manufacturer's recommendations for the maximum wattage allowed in lighting fixtures. Control lighting with switches placed at entrances and passageways.

Porches present unique lighting challenges. Open porches have few walls to reflect ambient light and are seldom used for tasks requiring specialized lighting. You should have a 60-watt incandescent outdoor lighting fixture on either side of an entry door, located 5 feet, 6 inches above the floor surface. Adding lighting fixtures at 10- to 15-foot intervals along porches provides enough ambient light for safety. If your porch ceiling is enclosed, you can add recessed fixtures. Porch lighting fixtures do not need to be rated for outdoor use if they are adequately protected by the porch roof—you can even use decorative fixtures, such as chandeliers. Have your outdoor fixtures controlled by switches placed on the wall next to each entry door leading to the porch. For nighttime security, you may want to include lights that are controlled by motion sensors.

Ceiling fans are a popular fixture because they make porch spaces comfortable when the weather is hot and air movement is minimal. Many types of ceiling fans include lights and are controlled either by pull chains or switches located inside the house. The minimum requirement for headroom beneath a ceiling fan typically is 80 inches.

Adding Lights and Fans

Adequate lighting allows you to maximize the enjoyment of your space. Most lighting schemes include ambient lighting for general purposes and task lighting for specific needs, such as reading or cooking. There also may be accent lighting to illuminate and highlight certain objects such as pieces of art. The more specific your goals and plans for the use of your new porch or sunroom, the better you'll be able to plan, select, and install the right lighting.

Enclosed sunrooms have lighting requirements typical to indoor living areas. Provide ambient lighting with recessed ceiling fixtures, track lighting, or wall sconces. Calculate the ambient lighting requirements in lumens—a measure of lighting output. Lumens are listed on the packages that contain lightbulbs, but not

MAKE A PLAN

Just because a sunroom boasts a lot of natural light doesn't mean it needs minimal lighting. Plan to include general, task, and accent lighting, so you can enjoy your sunroom even after the sun sets.

Planning the Budget

A workable budget usually is a compromise between all the great things you imagine for your finished project and what you're willing to spend to achieve your goals. Your first priority should be to set limits for the total amount of money you'll spend. As a guide, make two lists. One list should include everything you consider essential for your new space. The other list should be the extras—the amenities you'd like to have if there's money left over after you pay for essentials. Once you've developed your budget, stay committed to it. A commitment to your bottom line will help you make the difficult cost-cutting decisions if your project threatens to go over budget.

As you finalize your ideas and move toward construction, request bids from contractors and other professionals you're considering to complete the work. Convey both your goals and your budget to the professionals involved in the project. Once you receive bids, add a 5 to 10 percent cushion to the total figure to cover probable cost overruns and changes to your plans that may occur after construction has begun.

Though your budget should definitely include all of the essentials for your project,

MAKE A PLAN

Control costs by finalizing your plans before work begins. One of the biggest budget-blowers is changing your plans once work is under way. Make sure you spend plenty of time in the planning stage before leaping into construction. Changing the placement of a wall on paper may result in only minimal charges if you've hired a design professional to draw your plans. Changing the placement of a wall once construction has begun may be a major expense.

it is possible to save money by comparison shopping and researching alternatives. Some materials—such as certain natural stone tiles, for example—can be very expensive. Research flooring alternatives that replicate the look of the natural stone; you may find the look you want for substantially less per square foot. You may also consider doing some of the work yourself. Perhaps you can tackle minor surface regrading, as well as handle the clean-up and finish work, such as painting and installing trim.

SOURCES OF MONEY

Determining how you will finance your porch or sunroom project is a personal decision. Here are a few of the most common funding options:

- **Savings.** Rather than paying interest to a lending institution, you may want to borrow from yourself.
- **Home equity loan.** With this type of loan, you are borrowing against the equity you've built up in your home. Home equity rates and terms are fixed, so your payment each month over the term of the loan is the same. The terms for this type of loan are generally between five and 30 years. The amount you can borrow depends on factors such as your home's appraised or fair market value and the amount you still owe on any outstanding mortgage loans. The interest paid on this type of loan is generally tax deductible.
- **Home equity line of credit.** This is a form of revolving credit based on your home's value and the amount of equity you have. With this type of loan, you have the flexibility of borrowing as you go. Interest rates are variable, so monthly payments will vary.
- **Refinancing or cash-out mortgage loan.** Taking a cash-out mortgage loan allows you to refinance your mortgage for a higher overall amount than what you currently owe on your home. The amount depends on factors such as the accumulated equity in your home and the current value of your home. Interest rates are lower than home equity loans, but you will generally have to pay the standard closing costs.

The Basics of Building

Understanding construction keeps your projects efficient.

Knowing the fundamentals for construction allows you to establish effective communications with your architect, general contractor, and other professionals. Good communication helps to keep the job on time and on budget. If you do the work yourself, learning about the building process familiarizes you with materials and the sequence of events so you can make informed decisions.

Finding and hiring the right contractor for the job is also a process. Take the time to make sure the team you contract for the job is familiar with porch and sunroom construction and that you feel comfortable with their abilities and level of professionalism.

A porch or sunroom project has several phases. Knowing what to expect during each phase will help you prepare for the next step, enabling the project to proceed as smoothly as possible. Though the end result will certainly be worth it, some of the phases of building can be trying. Being prepared for the mess and disruption helps minimize potential frustrations.

Unless you are an accomplished do-it-yourselfer, the building process includes essentials such as getting bids, hiring a contractor, and signing written contracts. Understanding what each of these involves will help ensure you make the right choices and negotiate a fair contract.

Adding a front porch to this turn-of-the-20th-century home provided the visual substance and support the original home was lacking. The wraparound porch replaced a small concrete landing that was dwarfed by the home and property. The new porch works with the proportions of the home and creates plenty of space for relaxing with guests.

Window treatments give porches and sunrooms a touch of elegance and romance. They soften large amounts of hard glass surface, provide privacy, and help to control excessive light and glare. Roll-up shades, fabric curtains, and blinds made of split bamboo are functional while adding accents of personal style. For the longest-lasting window treatments, select mildew-resistant fabrics that can withstand repeated washings. Choose hardware constructed from brass, bronze, or stainless steel for outdoor durability.

Any traditional window treatment will work in a sunroom, but hot, bright sun can quickly fade the colors in fabrics that are not especially made to resist fading. On porches, billowing fabric curtains add swaths of color and a refined—yet fun—sense of style to living areas that are completely open to the outdoors.

Be creative in your approach to window treatments. Sheer cotton panels add a dreamy background, while cotton sheets make simple, low-cost curtains. They come in a variety of colors and prints, but as sheets aren't designed for direct exposure to sunlight, don't expect colors to last very long. Shower curtains also work well—they are durable, moisture-resistant, and have many colors and textures. Mosquito netting tied back as curtain panels on an open porch looks decorative, but becomes functional when enlisted into use. Split bamboo and matchstick blinds are popular choices—the natural wood tones blend readily with a variety of design schemes. Used on a porch, blinds made of wood should be coated with a clear, penetrating wood sealer prior to installation to prevent staining and mildew.

A valance lends a finishing touch to this sunroom dining area. If privacy and light control are issues, select a longer valance and attach window treatments that can be lowered—such as Roman shades or blinds—behind the valance.

Striped canvas awnings can be lowered for privacy, or to block sun, wind, and rain. Massive unpainted timbers provide a visual transition between the sheltered porch and the natural spaces beyond.

MAKE A PLAN

On an open porch, use fabric panels to give the illusion and privacy of walls, without their confining limitations. Lower the panels when you want to escape to an intimate retreat; raise them to let the sunshine and breezes flow through the porch. Depending on the effect you want, choose a gauzy fabric to billow in the breeze, or a heavier weight for a more tailored look.

Rugs

A painted floorcloth fashioned from a vinyl remnant anchors a seating area on this porch. Two coats of satin-finish polyurethane protect the surface. Old wicker chairs were revived with the same shade of warm tan exterior latex paint.

Rugs provide splashes of color and soften the look and feel of hard surface floorings such as ceramic tile or concrete. Area rugs anchor conversation and other furniture groupings on a porch or sunroom—position seating either entirely on or entirely off the rug. Versatile area rugs give you the option to quickly and easily change the look and feel of a space by moving or replacing them.

MAKE A PLAN

Area rugs crafted from synthetic mildew-resistant fibers are perfect for open porches and conservatories brimming with plants. Maintenance is easy: Simply hose off the rugs when they begin to show dirt or mud.

Although you can use any type of rug in a porch or sunroom, remember that these environments are prone to dirt and grime tracked in from the outdoors. Choose moderately priced dhurries, kilims, or woven rag

rugs that are colorful, durable, and easy to clean. Rugs of sisal or hemp are naturally resistant to moisture and have a casual appearance that blends well with most porch or sunroom groupings. Acrylic rugs provide an easy-care, fade-resistant surface covering. For high-traffic areas, select a piece of indoor-outdoor carpeting and have all the edges bound.

Because sisal accent rugs are typically inexpensive, try your hand at painting or dying one to create a personalized look for your porch or sunroom. Sisal accepts fabric dye and latex paint well. For painted rugs, apply nonyellowing floor wax to protect the paint from chipping. Painting a floorcloth is another do-it-yourself option for an inexpensive and colorful area rug ideal for a porch or sunroom. Start with a primed canvas, then apply latex paint in the design of your choice—use stencils or take a freehand approach. Add several coats of polyurethane to protect and seal the cloth. As needed, clean with mild soap and water.

MAKE A PLAN

Position an area rug to create a cozy conversation area. Choose rugs with patterns and colors that forgive dirt, and choose fibers and weaves that are sturdy enough to withstand heavy wear.

Grandmother's rag rug is a fitting floor covering for this cottage porch. A pink window box, watering can, and maple syrup bucket are whimsical, unexpected ways to introduce more of this lighthearted hue.

A plush area rug covers rustic decklike floorboards in this screen porch, offering foot-comforting softness in the seating area. Positioned in the center of the porch, the rug is protected from most harsh elements.

Houseplants for Sunrooms

A trio of plants and a paneled door screen create the perfect backdrop to a quiet reading corner in this cheerful sunroom. Grouping plants is similar to combining fabrics. Choose three varieties that offer a pleasing mix of color, shape, size, and texture. Here a small-leaf, frilly ivy serves counterpoint to the large, creamy leaves of a caladium. A tall, full plant such as a palm provides height.

Conservatories were traditionally used in 18th- and 19th-century England to extend the growing season and to display plants. Sunrooms and conservatories now take on a much broader role, serving as a sun-drenched space for virtually any purpose from cooking to bathing to entertaining. Plants remain a natural choice to enhance sunrooms. Lush greenery helps to create a tranquil retreat just as much as the right furnishings, fabrics, and colors.

If you are new to gardening and plants, start with an easy-to-grow selection. Many plants survive, even thrive, with little watering and fertilizing. Though it's critical to select plants whose light requirements match the lighting conditions in your sunroom, beyond that, consider the decorating scheme and architecture of your space when you select and display plants. For a charming cottage-style sunroom, look for delicate ferns and ivies. For a more streamlined contemporary design, choose plants with elegant lines such as bromeliads or snake plants. Cacti and succulents enhance a southwestern décor. In addition to the plants themselves, consider, too, potential containers. Select pot colors, materials, and finishes that complement the style and color scheme of your sunroom.

Group plants for greater impact. Position plants on shelves and decorative plant stands. Use multiple containers of the same plant, or combine a variety of plants that possess a colorful variety of foliage, interesting textures, shapes, and heights. Look for plants that feature flowers that coordinate with the color scheme of your room. Position a large plant or indoor tree in the corner for dramatic flair. Just make sure you provide enough space for growth.

To keep plants flourishing, begin by choosing plants with light requirements that match your sunroom environment. Remember that light will be most intense directly on a windowsill. Use an enriched potting soil to repot plants in new containers. Plants require periodic repotting—typically every couple of years—to maintain healthy growth. Follow the water and fertilization recommendations. Avoid overwatering. Water at the edge of a container rather than pouring water directly on the foliage. Give plants a quarter-turn each week to prevent spindly growth on one side of the plant.

A small side table is an ideal spot to group a collection of flowering plants including miniature roses and African violets. The colors and shapes of the flowers and pots work with the design scheme of the sunroom.

A small potting area built along one wall of this sunroom is a convenient spot for dividing perennials, arranging cut flowers, and storing supplies. If necessary, the area rug can be moved and the concrete floor hosed off.

The Basics of Landscaping

Harmonize your porch or sunroom with its surroundings.

The appeal of an inviting front porch or sunroom derives from the structure and its furnishings, but also from what surrounds it. Landscaping around your porch creates curb appeal. As you enjoy your porch or sunroom, your enjoyment will come both from the space itself as well as what you see as you gaze beyond to the surrounding landscape.

When planning your porch or sunroom, include appropriate landscaping concepts that will help put the finishing touches on your addition. Plan foundation plantings as an attractive cover for tall foundations that otherwise look bare. Consider planting even the most basic of gardens to provide an attractive transition between your porch or sunroom and the surrounding area.

Just as you took time to gather ideas for your new porch or sunroom and then reviewed those with a design professional to meet your goals for the new space, take time to look through books and magazines and to visit nurseries and garden centers for landscaping ideas. Consult with a landscape architect or landscape designer for ideas or for a complete landscape plan. The landscaping will be an enduring part of your home. Thoughtful planning should provide a landscape that will offer years of enjoyment and satisfaction.

The front porch addition to this 1940s cottage gives the house character and provides plenty of room for relaxing and casual entertaining. Fresh landscaping and a new flagstone walkway were essential to providing the curb appeal this home now delivers.

Critical to developing a landscape plan that will work for you is an assessment of what is needed to provide an attractive transition from your new porch or sunroom to the surrounding area. If you have a tall, bare foundation, for example, you'll need foundation plantings that fill in the gaps and soften the lines.

Look at the plans for your new porch or sunroom. Note how the addition will impact your yard and current landscaping. Foundation shrubs and surrounding gardens may be removed to make way for the sunroom, leaving bare dirt around the new addition. Account for these changes in the landscape plan.

Remember that landscaping includes more than plants, shrubs, and trees. Consider hardscapes—permanent non-plant features—such as walks, paths, fences, walls, and patios. New French doors that lead from your sunroom to the yard offer an opportunity for a flagstone path to replace an existing expanse of grass. Perhaps a walkway needs to be moved to tie in with a new entry created by a front porch addition. Just as you selected materials for your new porch or sunroom that blend seamlessly with your existing home, plan to use hardscape materials that harmonize with both.

Use landscaping elements to create the ideal environment for your new porch or sunroom. If the neighbors have a clear view into the screen porch you envision as a private retreat, design a "wall" of evergreens to attractively block the view and shelter your space.

Style is another important consideration when defining your landscaping plans. The architecture and color scheme of your home, your personal tastes, experience with plants and gardening, and lifestyle should all impact your choices for the landscape. Consider the style of your home. A charming cottage with a quaint front porch would be better complemented by an informal garden featuring long-blooming flowers, than formal clipped hedges. Look at the color combinations used on your home. Purple and fuchsia blooms may look jarring against a red brick facade. Personal taste is important. Spend time strolling your neighborhood and noting the varieties, shapes, and colors of trees, shrubs, flowers, and grasses that you like and that look striking with your style of home. Take into account your lifestyle as you plan landscaping. If you are always on the go and want to spend the few precious moments at home with your feet propped up enjoying a glass of cool lemonade on the porch, select low-care shrubs and trees to landscape around the porch.

Combining existing trees and shrubs with new foundation plantings creates a pleasing transition between the front walk and yard, and this porch. Tall plants and trees anchor the sides of the porch and direct attention to the entry.

MAKE A PLAN

Before finalizing shrub or tree selections, read the plant tags for expected mature height and width. That cute little shrub you adore at the nursery may quickly outgrow its intended space and block views. Select dwarf varieties if necessary.

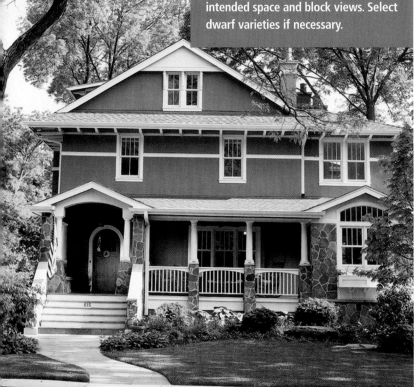

Creating Transitions with Landscaping

Porches and sunrooms are transition areas that blend the indoors and the outdoors. Creating a transition between the new space and the outdoors is just as much about the view and movement from the porch or sunroom to the yard beyond as it is about looking toward the house from the exterior. (See Foundation Plantings, pages 158–159 for information about creating a nice view from the exterior toward your home.) With proper planning, the area beyond your porch or sunroom becomes a natural extension of the space. The planning begins with the design of the space itself. Proper design of the room includes entryways from your home to the porch or sunroom, and from the space to the outdoors. Landscaping the outside area surrounding the new porch or sunroom expands your potential uses of the space, and adds to your enjoyment of it.

Use hardscapes. Plan patios, decks, paths, or walkways that extend from the entrances of the porch or sunroom. An adjacent patio or deck allows traffic to easily flow indoors and outdoors and provides additional options for large gatherings. Paths or walkways that lead from the porch or sunroom to surrounding gardens encourage you and your visitors to enjoy the pleasures of the outdoors and minimize the tracking of dirt and debris into your home.

Consider the sights and sounds. You will most likely spend much of your time on the porch or sunroom gazing out into the yard. Perhaps you are fortunate to have sited the space to take advantage of a breathtaking view such as a distant mountain range. More likely, your gaze falls on your neighbor's house. Create your own visual interest by adding a garden, trellis, or outdoor sculpture. Install a bubbling fountain just outside the sunroom's French doors. The soothing gurgle of water will provide pleasant background sounds.

Create continuity. The transition between your home, porch, or sunroom, and the landscape beyond will feel and look more natural if you choose materials, colors, and plants that are related. If you plant a garden within viewing distance, include a few of the same plants as you used in the foundation plantings surrounding the sunroom. If your porch has a brick floor, install a brick path connecting the porch to the yard.

A stone walkway with wide steps was carved into a stone wall and steep slope to create an easy segue to the porch steps. Flowering plants neatly fill the space between the foundation and walkway. Positioning plants that will stay short in front of the porch ensures views will remain open as the plants mature.

Welcoming Front Porches

Even porticos—the smallest of front porches—can serve as an inviting entry to your home. Augmented with cheerful flowers blooming in the gardens along the path to the porch, in baskets hanging from the eaves, pots along the steps and landing, and in window boxes, the entry of this home offers a charming welcome to visitors.

The front porch is most likely the first thing that visitors notice when they arrive at your home. A well-planned porch and surrounding area welcomes guests and guides them to the main entry of your home. Plants soften as well as enhance the architectural lines of the porch foundation, walkway, and steps. When planning the landscaping for a front porch, consider how the plantings and hardscapes work with the architecture of the house and porch. If you have a formal home and traditional portico offering entryway shelter, a pair of carefully pruned boxwoods in containers flanking the front door will continue the formality. If you have a sweeping front porch that spans the length of the house, develop a landscape plan for the length of the porch.

When space is available, use the porch as stage to feature containers and hanging baskets of flowers. Coordinate the colors of foliage and flowers, and their containers, with the palette of fabrics and furnishings on your porch. Fragrant plants are ideal for front-porch containers. They provide a pleasant aroma for guests and the natural

MAKE A PLAN

The most successful landscape plans for front porches take into account the conditions of the site. Pay attention to the exposure of the area and choose plants whose light requirements match. If deep eaves limit the amount of water that reaches the soil, choose plants that prefer it dry.

This front porch offers a cozy sitting area enhanced with potted and hanging baskets of flowers, as well as lush vegetation that screens the view and provides privacy. Oversize stone planters on each of the porch columns serve as manageable places for seasonal flowers.

perfume infuses the house every time the door is opened.

If you have a walkway leading to your front porch, consider bordering it with plants that are inviting to the touch. Ferns, soft-needled conifers, and some ornamental grasses are good options. Avoid planting thorny or spiky plants right along the pathway and porch railing. Stray stems may scratch guests.

Shrubs and other plants positioned near the base of a porch or sunroom conceal the bare foundation, creating a pleasing transition between the house and landscape. Foundation plantings shouldn't be limited to a row of shrubs. That formation simply separates the structure from the rest of the landscape instead of tying the two together. Select plants with a variety of heights creating a gradual transition from foundation to groundcover. Or tier the ground during grading to provide the transition from vertical house to horizontal lawn; then use similar height plants on each level.

Staggering the heights of plants in front of a porch makes this an attractive foundation planting and effectively conceals the foundation. Repetition of several colors and plants throughout the garden and in the pots and hanging baskets on the porch yields continuity.

MAKE A PLAN

Put foundation plantings far enough away from your porch or sunroom so they won't be in the way when you need to work on the exterior. Position shrubs so exterior electrical outlets are accessible.

Incorporate variety. Successful foundation plantings incorporate a variety of colors, shapes, and textures that coordinate with the home, porch or sunroom, and adjacent gardens. Avoid planting one of everything you like. Instead, group similar plants for maximum impact.

Consider shape. Look at the plant tag for the natural shape of the plant. For a formal look, don't select informal plants with graceful, arching branches and expect to prune it into a compact globe. Select a more compact, geometrically shaped shrub.

Pay attention to size. Don't underestimate the mature size of a plant. You can't always prune a plant to maintain the size you desire. Though some plants are ideal for heavy shearing, others will soon look unattractive, or get unwieldy despite your efforts. Provide enough room for plants to spread. Use mature size information on the plant tag to position plants. Though the new landscape, flowers and shrubs may look too small for the spacing. Be patient, they will be ideal after a few seasons of growth.

Plant in layers. Nearest to the porch or sunroom position the tallest layer of shrubs or small, ornamental trees. Shrubs will provide better foundation coverage because they become more dense and full than trees. In front of the tallest layer, plant medium-height dwarf varieties of shrubs and perennials. The outermost layer should consist of groundcover or short perennials. Fill in with annuals to provide instant seasonal color. Three-layer foundation plantings require beds about 6 to 10 feet wide, depending on the specific plants you choose.

COMMON FOUNDATION SHRUBS

Though many shrubs can work in a foundation planting, here are some of the most common and attractive:

Azalea (many varieties)	Dwarf Yew (Taxus spp.)
Bird's Nest Spruce (Picea abies)	Inkberry (Ilex glabra)
Boxwood (Buxus spp.)	Japanese Barberry
Cotoneaster (Cotoneaster spp.)	(Berberis thunbergii)
Dwarf Arborvitae (Thuja spp.)	Japanese Holly (Ilex crenata)
Dwarf False Cypress	Juniper (Juniperus spp.)
(Chamaecyparis spp.)	Mugo Pine (Pinus mugo)
Dwarf Korean Lilac (Syringa meyeri)	Spirea (Spiraea spp.)

Index

Page numbers in **_bold italic_** type indicate photographs.

Index